MW00830299

FLIGHT LINE

The Adventures of a Vietnam Veteran
AC-130 Crew Chief

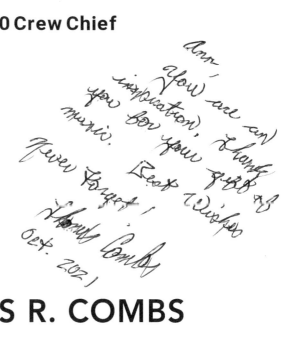

THOMAS R. COMBS

HELLGATE PRESS   ASHLAND, OREGON

FLIGHT LINE

©2018 Thomas R. Combs

Published by Hellgate Press
(An imprint of L&R Publishing, LLC)

Hellgate Press
PO Box 3531
Ashland, OR 97520
email: info@hellgatepress.com

Interior & Cover Design: L. Redding

ISBN: 978-1-954163-14-0

Printed and bound in the United States of America
First edition 10 9 8 7 6 5 4 3 2 1

This book is dedicated to my father, Carroll C. Combs, and
my mother, Constance M. Combs. Thank you for giving me life, love
and a childhood filled with fond memories of family, friends, joy and
laughter. I regret that my dad did not live long enough to see me grow
into adulthood and become a husband and father modeled after his
example. My mom lived a long and wonderful life and was able to read
my early manuscript. She became a mother and a father to all four of her
sons and did an exquisite job of parenting. When in doubt I will always
ask myself, "How would Mom or Dad act?" I love you both forever!

WE WERE IN A SMALL VALLEY WITH RENEGADE TANKS and rocket propelled grenade launchers on both sides of us! I'm sure I was holding my breath as we moved from the taxi-way to the end of the runway. Wasting no time, the pilot brought our engines to full throttle and released the brakes. The C-130 practically jumped into the air! We were not "out of the woods" yet, but I was feeling better as we flew higher.

CONTENTS

Prologue

I N THE SUMMER OF 1996, THE ONE-HALF SCALE Vietnam Veterans
Memorial (known as the traveling wall) came to Washington State.
Over that three-day weekend, I visited the memorial three times. I had
always wondered where on the wall, were the more than fifty names of
my comrades and friends. Like many veterans before me, the simple act
of touching those names reawakened old memories and emotions. It was
then that I decided to put some of these memories and feelings on paper.
I have tried my best to highlight both the good and the bad memories.
The story I have told is true. Let me apologize in advance for any
mistakes I have made, for none is intentional. Some memories are like
yesterday's news, they have never left my subconscious mind. Others
began to flow as my story unfolded on paper.

It is difficult to express the entire scope of my experiences. I can
vividly remember the sights, the sounds, the smells, the people and the
places, but it is hard to adequately convey all of that in a short story such
as this. Nothing can replace the experience of "being there." For those
readers, parts of this story may ring true. For others without the benefit
of the experience, I hope that at least a mental picture emerges to provide
a sense of what it was like. My story is only one of thousands to be told.
I sincerely hope you enjoy reading it.

Certainly no project such as this can be fulfilled without the assistance
of others. I would like to thank my wife, Ruth, for her comments and
suggestions during the early stages of development. I love you! A
profound thank you goes to my family and friends, for giving their love

and support over the years. I send my enduring love to my daughter, Tracy. She was, of course, too young at the time to remember these events. Love to my son, Jesse, who placed time and talent into the formatting of this book. My children are my greatest achievements! Thank you Jason, for reading my manuscript, and thank you Tristan, Tanner, Ryder, Addison and Alexander for being born.

I remember a number of years ago when Jesse was in school and studying the Vietnam War. He asked a few questions, yet disputed that I was, in fact, a Vietnam veteran! Deep inside I knew then my story should be told, if for no other reason than to set the record straight.

This story is dedicated to all of those who played a part in my short career in the U. S. Air Force. To my instructors, who paved the way with their expertise and to the air and ground crews who shared many of my unique experiences. To the many professionals I had the privilege of working and flying with during these four years, especially those who became close friends. Finally with great pride and honor, to the lost crews of three AC-130 gunships, serial numbers 044, 043 and 490: Maj. Ramsower, Maj. Brauner, Capt. Castillo, Capt. Halpin, Capt. Miller, Maj. Stephenson, Capt. Wanzel, Capt. Young, SSgt. Caniford, Msgt. Paulson, SSgt. Pearce, A1C. Simmons, SSgt. Smith, Sgt. Todd, Maj. Ayers, SSgt. Cole, Capt. Danielson, Capt. Gilbert, Maj. Harrison, Sgt. Hunt, SSgt. Klinke, SSgt. Nyhof, Sgt. Lehrke, Msgt. Mercer, SSgt. Newman, Capt. Birch, A1C. Fenter, Tsgt. Fuller, A1C Reaid, Maj. Walsh, Tsgt. Winningham, Capt. Hart, Capt. Kroboth, Capt. Lagerwall, Capt. Liles, Lt. Mac-Donald, Maj. Meder, Capt. Dickens, and Sgt. Elliott. I am honored to have served with you.

ONE

Basic Training

"MR. COMBS IS SCHEDULED FOR DRAFT INDUCTION on September 15th." With these words, my fate was sealed. It was mid April 1969. I was sitting in the downtown Seattle office of the Selective Service System attempting to gain a student deferment. It wasn't working! The overweight gray-haired lady looked at me and smiled. Her huge arm dropped my folder down on the table with a slap. She was enjoying seeing me squirm. There were others in the room with us, but I only remember her face. In a daze, I wandered out of the office and back to my car. What was I going to do? If I waited and did nothing I would be drafted into the Army or Marines. I didn't like the odds. I knew that thousands of American men had already died in Vietnam. These brave men were from all branches of the military. I was not eager to go.

In the days following, I looked into the Reserves, any Reserves - Coast Guard, Navy and Air Force. They all had a two-year waiting list. Bob Ittes was a high school friend of mine facing the same situation. I had focused on the Air Force as the best possible selection and tried to convince Bob. A few days later he and I talked with the Air Force recruiter in Seattle. Yes, we could go under the "buddy system!" We could join up and serve together the entire six years (four were active and two were inactive reserve). It sounded good under the circumstances, so we did. After a day of aptitude tests we were told to hang out and enjoy the summer. We could expect to start Basic Training in mid August.

I had discussed my options with my high school sweetheart, Denise. We both realized my enlistment meant I was going away for at least four years. She was against the war, and both of us knew people from high school who enlisted or had been drafted. Some of those guys didn't come home. We spent long hours talking about our future together, and her status changed from girlfriend to fiancé.

Denise and I were married in early June and set up house in a small Bellevue apartment. We watched like millions of people around the world as the United States landed a man on the moon. I felt proud to soon be a part of the U.S. Air Force. Somewhere in upstate New York, a huge outdoor concert was taking place. It was called Woodstock. As summer progressed, Denise worked, and I worried.

All too soon late August came around. Bob and I were scheduled for our physicals. What an experience that was! Anyone who has gone through it will know. All forms of life seemed to be gathered in that place... some real weirdos. Most of us, I think, were just scared. After the physical, those of us who had signed up were sworn in with a formal oath. Rather than go home for the night and fly out the next day, they "ordered" us onto a bus and we were driven to the YMCA in Seattle to spend the night. I had said my goodbyes already and stayed awake most of the night listening to fights and shouting and noise outside my dreary room.

Early the next morning, we were herded onto a bus and taken to Sea-Tac Airport for the flight to Lackland Air Force Base in San Antonio, Texas. The flight went smoothly, all things considered. The pilot announced a contest over the intercom system. A prize awarded to the person who could predict our arrival time in San Antonio. He gave us our altitude, heading, speed and distance, as well as head winds, etc. We all wrote our names and estimates on sheets of paper. I won! With a complete shot-in-the-dark guess, my estimate was the closest of everyone else on board the airplane. I received a deck of cards with the airline logo on them.

As we casually filed off the plane and into the terminal, I could hear shouts in the distance becoming louder and louder. It was the Air Force

DIs (Drill Instructors). We were told to get against the wall, shut-up and look straight ahead. Oh shit! They roughed us up just enough to let us know who was in charge. The DIs picked out a few guys with long hair and some with a smile or a smirk on their face. They shouted loudly at these guys right here in the airport lobby in front of astonished civilians. The people walked past briskly no doubt glad they were not with us. I watched them, wishing I could step out of line and walk away. We were ordered onto an Air Force bus and driven to Lackland Air Base. It was dark and close to midnight. We rode for about an hour in complete silence. It seemed like ten hours. Once on base, we were herded into what the DIs called "Hell's Kitchen."

"Look straight ahead, no talking," shouted the DIs. We were standing shoulder to shoulder, shuffling through the line. Approaching each section, our meal was thrown at our trays by scared Airmen. Each portion arrived with a smack. We sat four to a table, looking straight ahead, trying to eat. The DIs went through us with shouts of, "Hold your fork straight, sit up, and finish your food!" Any food on our trays had to be finished. We were given maybe three minutes to eat, and then forced back on the bus. We were taken to a newer two-story, large barracks complex and ordered out of the bus. They lined us up according to our height. We were in four lines of about fifteen guys each. Next, line-by-line we marched up to our barracks. Once we were inside, the instructor assigned us to individual bunks and lockers. One last shout came from the doorway, "Lights out!" I lay there listening to the unfamiliar sounds wondering what I had gotten myself into.

At 4:30 in the morning, the lights came on and the DIs started rumbling through blaring a referee's whistle. This became the routine for the next six weeks.

We were given haircuts, uniforms and physicals. I was not prepared for the very hot shaver that crisscrossed my head in seconds. The barber had been using this shaver all day, and he seemed to enjoy the added discomfort placed on each recruits' head.

We walked a straight line into a building early one morning, going in one end and out the other. I could see the others coming out now, as I was going in. Some of the recruits where bending over and throwing up. Others were rubbing their arms. Shots! We were given injections on both sides by medics in white uniforms as we shuffled through. Some of the doctors used needles while others used an air gun. I made it through okay, but not everybody did.

We learned how to march in formation and we underwent PT (physical training) for hours every day, in the 105-degree Texas sun. The Air Force had set up a flag system to tell us if it was too hot to do our PT. Yellow meant caution. Red was supposed to mean no physical activity. To our Drill Instructor, Red was Green. We ran, then marched and exercised for hours near the tiny shadow of that red flag almost every day. If we were the only Flight remaining outside in the Texas sun that day, then the better off our Flight would be. Usually, we stayed long after the other Flights had left. Our drill instructor did make us strong and proud.

"Smoke 'em if you got 'em." The DI announced one morning. These six little words would make me a smoker. Occasionally, the DIs would allow the smokers to break from formation and sit on the grass to enjoy a brief smoke break. Those not afflicted with the deadly habit had to stand at parade-rest and remain in formation. Smokers carried their cigarettes in a pack-size blue box. The box had adjustable straps allowing the user to discreetly attach it to the ankle. (We could not make use of our pockets as we were expected to maintain a smooth uniform profile.) After bumming some cigarettes for a couple of days, I purchased those blue boxes for my own use, along with a pack of Half-n-Half cigarettes. This brand was pipe tobacco in cigarette form and very strong. I purchased two boxes at the Base Exchange. The extra box would be used to carry my razor and soap. Cigarettes were on one ankle and soap on the other. I know it sounds odd but we did this for a very good reason. Each recruit had a locker next to his bed in the barracks. In each locker we were expected to keep socks, underwear, soap and various other items neatly lined up with no dust or wrinkles etc., which would result in demerits and a severe chewing out by our DI. Someone came up with the idea of having 'show' pieces in the locker unused, while the actual utensils were kept in the box strapped to our ankles. This way when the DI inspected our razor for example, it would always be clean and spotless. So, we marched daily in the heat with our toiletries and cigarettes firmly attached to our ankles hidden by our fatigue pants. Some guys carried extras to keep socks and underwear in as well. If you were to listen real hard, you could probably have heard the distinct rattling sound near the ground as we marched past.

We had classroom instruction on Air Force history and the uniform code of military justice. All of our personal belongings had been taken away (including my deck of cards). We slowly became a single unit known in the Air Force as a "flight."

The Flights became a squadron and a squadron became a wing, etc. I tried to stay clean and not make waves. The DIs were in my face regardless but less so than the others. Then it happened. One afternoon after marching throughout the grounds, we were given two minutes to run upstairs, change into our PT shorts with canteens and back down and in proper formation. As always, it's a mad dash of sixty guys going to the same place, doing the same thing. I got back in time and was breathing a sigh of relief as the DIs were walking through the formation and shouting at a few unlucky souls who forgot to remove rings or watches. To my horror, I glanced down and discovered my watch still on my wrist. With a subtle move (I thought), I slipped it off and held it in my closed fist. The DIs walked up and down our flight and came to the front and asked if anyone else still had on jewelry. I kept quiet and stared straight ahead. I should have known by his questions that he knew, but I did not.

"Airman Basic Combs front and center!" Oh shit, I've had it. I took one step back and executed a crisp left face. I then walked to the end of the row, turned right face to the front and saluted the DI just as we had been trained to do. "Airman Combs, what is in your hand? He boomed. "Sir…my watch, sir!" I replied. (Sir was always the first word out of our mouths.) He berated me in front of the rest of our flight and screamed in my ear, for not owning up to his earlier question. The instructor snatched my watch from my hand slipping it into his pocket. I was ordered back in formation and we all marched out to the PT field to join up with the other Flights.

After running our two miles around the track, our instructor who was standing with a group of other DIs, ordered me over to them. As I stood at attention before them, my instructor berated me again as other DIs joined in. As part of our punishment, those of us who had forgotten to remove rings or watches were ordered to forego lunch and remain in the field. We were ordered to pick up rocks. We were told by the DI that he would come back in an hour, and of the four of us, whoever had the biggest pile could rejoin the flight. The other three would remain another hour and the process repeated. An hour later the DI came out, judged our four piles of rocks and declared one to be the largest and that recruit left. Another hour went by and out he came again and declared another winner and left. Now only two of us remained and the rocks were getting scarce. Both of us started removing rocks from the other two piles and ours grew dramatically. After three hours in the sun, the DI returned and said we were tied (mine was much larger). We were forced to drop and do thirty pushups in the hot dusty field before our DI was satisfied. We were told to rejoin the group and our punishment was ended. A week later, the DI ordered me to report to his office. After saluting and moving to parade rest, we locked eyes. The DI reached into his drawer and slowly pulled out my watch. Dropping it onto his desk, he said I had handled my punishment well and could now have my watch back. I reached down and immediately slid it onto my left wrist. Everything was nice-nice for a few moments when out of the blue, he offered me the squad leader position. I declined the promotion and he flew into a rage! In a small way, I felt I had gotten back at him.

****

"You are all going to Vietnam," the DI announced one day, sending ripples of doom through us. We were tested on aptitude to see what career we were best suited for. We fired the M-16 rifle and I hit twenty-nine of thirty, earning a marksmanship ribbon. Not bad, I thought, since I had never fired a real gun before!

We grew as a tight-knit group and became a team helping each other with our lessons and marching formations. We completed the obstacle course including a gas chamber, where many of the guys coughed and puked. The course was a lot like the back woods of Washington. I was eager to do well on the obstacle course and did. I had been running and climbing through the woods most of my twenty years. I didn't set any records, but I passed up many of the guys in my Flight. Towards the end of our six weeks we started singing in cadence as we marched. My pride as a member of the U.S. Air Force grew.

We were given a day pass to roam the base at will, so Bob Ittes and I went roller-skating and we really felt alive. For weeks we had been under constant supervision. Just being able to walk somewhere alone was a special treat.

One night we were crowded into a room and watched the new Selective Service lottery system on TV. I probably would have been called up under that system as well.

The DIs were warming up to us little by little as we progressed. One afternoon, we were told we would have a GI party. I actually thought he meant chips and punch to reward our efforts. Instead we marched upstairs to the latrine and were given toothbrushes. We spent hours on our hands and knees making the latrine shine. The DI barely gave the room a glance when he poked his head through the door and told us to knock off for the day. He didn't even look! Some party that turned out to be, I thought.

Just when I thought we had escaped the dreaded KP duty, our DI came charging through the barracks one morning picking various recruits, seemingly at random. As he pointed to me he shouted for us to "fall out!" About twenty of us marched in the morning cold to the kitchen and turned over to the mess sergeant. To him we must have looked like criminals or misfits because he treated us as such. He never spoke, he shouted. We were ordered to perform various tasks and driven all day by this supreme asshole. My first task was to break up about one hundred pieces of chicken lying in huge vats. They were cold… almost frozen and produced edges that cut my hands. I did this for two hours. Then the sergeant grabbed two of us by the collar taking us to the front of the mess hall. He continued to shout at every one as we passed by. I was to pass out trays as the first large group of Airmen began to pass through for breakfast. After the first meal we had to clean tables and scrub the floors. Prior to lunch, I had to (believe it or not) peel potatoes. Like the chicken, the potatoes were very cold. Working with them for hours I began to lose the feeling in my hands. I ducked out every so often and hid in one of the stalls of the latrine. I knew if the sergeant-from-hell came in he wouldn't know who was in the stall. He did come barging in a couple of times, but never looked at who was inside. I managed to avoid about an hour's work this way. Hey, my hands hurt.

After dinner I was assigned wash duty. As the recruits finished their meal they were to gently drop their trays with us through an opening in the wall. That is what we were taught and that is what I had always done, but not these guys. As I turned from the sink, I got hit in the shoulder by a flying tray! A group from another flight passed through and thought it would be funny to give us grief. They tossed the trays through the window aiming at us. Food was flying all over as well and these guys were just laughing as they ran out. I noticed they had a stripe on each arm. That meant these guys were done with basic and about to ship out. Where are the DIs when you need them? It was one of the longest days of Basic Training for me. After that I developed a new respect for the poor souls who were on KP. As I passed through during my meals, I went out of my way sometimes to offer an encouraging word to those who were enduring their own day in hell. The mess sergeant was unmatched in his ability to arouse anger in some. Others he drove to tears. He was a colossal jerk. Fortunately, our six weeks of Basic Training were coming to an end, and our follow-on assignments were forthcoming.

"I am going to be a jet mechanic," I said as my orders arrived. Others were also getting their duty assignments to whichever technical school handled their specialty. My buddy Bob was going to be a mechanic on reciprocal engines, the old piston type. The school for both of us was at Sheppard Air Force Base in Wichita Falls, Texas.

We had a group picture taken of our Flight with our DI proudly at our side. He was a dead ringer for Hoss Cartwright of "Bonanza" fame. We were promoted from Airman Basic to Airman and could now sew on a stripe. We had our last haircut (we had one each week) and said our goodbyes, as we all scattered to the winds of technical schools. A handful of us were going to Sheppard AFB and we gathered with other newly minted Airmen for the bus ride north. I plopped down on my duffle bag next to an Airman from another Flight and introduced myself. His name was John Forsberg and we were both assigned to the same school. Little did I know that this was the beginning of many long and exciting adventures together.

FLIGHT LINE

TWO

Technical School

"**P**ING!" WHAT WAS THAT? "PING!" WE HEARD IT AGAIN. We had arrived at Sheppard AFB and in the hot Texas sun had the windows of the bus down all the way. "Hey, ping, yeah, you guys in the bus, Welcome to Sheppard." Ping was the sound of our hair growing back and the nickname of those of us fresh out of Basic Training. Judging by the length of hair on the heads of our welcoming committee, these guys had not been here long. We were assigned barracks and settled in for the night.

Each morning, my new group (jet mechanics) would assemble together outside the squadron orderly room for roll call. Our breathing was visible in the chilly morning air. Once all the names were called, we marched the five or six blocks to the flight line hangers. With no DIs around, we were marched by our squad leaders, and marching was jazzed up with a turn of the shoulder, a hoo-ahh response to their orders or a skip step when turning, etc. It was actually kind of fun. We also sang in cadence and had some pretty ripe lyrics.

"This aircraft gentleman, is a C-130A," said the instructor early one morning. Now I saw for the first time, the aircraft that I would be trained to maintain. It was huge! The aircraft had four turboprop engines. These were jet engines that through a reduction gear, turned three-bladed props on each engine. The C-130 wingspan was over 132 feet. The airplane was just less than 100 feet long. From here on the ground it was about

40 feet up to the top of the tail. The C-130 was a powerful four-engine transport and was used by the Air Force for a multitude of rolls. They could take off and land on dirt strips, the instructor told us. They were used to retrieve space capsules or drop commandos across enemy lines. Some were outfitted with skis to land in snow and ice. And yes, the instructor added the C-130 was being used heavily in the Vietnam War.

Tech school was a fourteen-week course that covered absolutely every facet of maintaining a C-130. Our classroom was a big hangar that was converted for our use. The Air Force had provided us with elaborate mock-ups of the systems we would learn about. Our training would provide us with hands-on knowledge of the electrical system, fuel system, hydraulics, avionics, engines, pneumatics, landing gear and airframe. We also made use of the "A" model C-130 parked on the ramp outside the hangar.

After the second week, my wife, Denise, and brother, Mick, drove down from Seattle. Wives were allowed now that Basic Training was over, and what a welcome sight. We found a small duplex apartment a few miles from base and set up house. Mick flew back to Seattle and left us his '67 Mustang to use. How many brothers do you know that would do something like that? Man, I was hot stuff!

This simple act changed everything. Not living in the barracks meant not marching to class each morning. Having a car meant I could drive to the hanger and park. After class I simply drove away watching in my rear-view mirror as the rest of the guys lined up for their march back to the barracks. Sorry guys. Yes, a few of my friends hitched a ride now and again. The Mustang was definitely status. Each morning as I drove through the main gate, the uniformed guard saluted me! I began to have a life again.

We had friends over for dinners and weekend parties. Some Airmen in my class were married as well, although we were definitely the minority. They also brought their wives to stay. On base it was all military spit and polish, but off base it was more relaxed. Finally, I could enjoy home cooked meals, TV and my stereo. I bought a debut record of a new sounding group called Santana. The Latin percussion knocked me out, and "Soul Sacrifice" was my favorite song.

Our little duplex also had the distinction of resting no further than ten feet from two sets of railroad tracks. Sleep did not always come easy those cold Texas nights. Trains rumbled by at all hours day and night.

Here in tech school the emphasis was on neatly starched fatigues. The squad leaders held daily inspections looking for reasons to write us up for extra duty. I didn't want to play dorm guard so I looked the part. On weekends Denise would go through bottle after bottle of spray starch, making my uniform stand in the corner...alone. Everyone tried to out-starch the other. It sort of got out of hand after a while, but we did look sharp.

School was interesting and challenging. We had tests every Friday. I looked forward to each week's lessons, and I became knowledgeable of just about every square inch of a C-130A aircraft. Throughout the aircraft, virtually every nut and bolt was safety wired. We learned right away that when we tore something down and rebuilt it, to make sure it stayed together; we were to safety wire everything. This connected the bolts to each other in a way that a loose bolt would only tighten the other as it loosened. By being interconnected like this, no individual bolt could loosen itself more than one half of a rotation. It was clever I thought and of course it worked! The whole airplane was a master of engineering. I was impressed and proud to be a part of it.

We spent a week learning all about the ground power units, the B-1 hydraulic stands, towing equipment and all the extra support materials needed to maintain this airplane. These would become the tools of my trade.

Sheppard was also home to a squadron of Vietnamese Air Force or VNAF pilots in training. These young Vietnamese would soon be their countries first line of defense. They kept mostly to themselves. However, on occasion they would come through our hanger and participate in maintenance exercises. Of course, they spoke little English, and we spoke no Vietnamese.

One day, as we were on a break outside the hangar, a Huey helicopter landed and came nearby to refuel. Something went wrong, and before we knew it, the chopper exploded into flames! The two pilots were killed instantly (they shouldn't have been in the chopper during refueling to begin with). I believe they were VNAF pilots. They became casualties of a war thousands of miles away. Back in the classroom we talked about safety and what can go wrong if we don't pay attention. The Huey explosion got my attention for personal reasons.

My oldest brother, Jack, was an Army pilot. He had just completed a combat tour flying Hueys in Vietnam. He earned The Distinguished Flying Cross and a Purple Heart among others for valor, flying into hot LZs and evacuating wounded GIs. He will forever be a hero to me! Jack, his wife Dianne and their little daughter Angel were stationed on an Army post nearby. One day he called to say he was coming up to see me; we were going to spend the weekend together. I arranged to meet him at the base bowling alley, and I was sure to stay indoors, as I was not quite sure if I was expected to salute him or not. He was a Captain in the Army and I was unsure about the proper protocol in these situations. Would he expect a salute or would he scoff at me if I did? Maybe he would think I was mocking him if I executed a crisp one. As it was, he showed up out of uniform and he was just my big brother. What a relief!

We had a great weekend together. He took me flying in a helicopter trainer. I had absolute confidence in his flying abilities and he amazed me with his command of the chopper's controls. We flew around for fifteen or twenty minutes before venturing over to an old Army airfield a few miles away. Below us I could see a couple of dilapidated hangers and a small control tower. The grass was growing along the unused runway, and old used equipment was strewn about. Here at 300 feet above the abandoned airstrip he taught me how to hover. I kept pulling us up higher and backward. My hands gripped the controls tightly, and I was keying the mike button! Jack got me to relax and I settled in to fly and hover that little helicopter. At least I flew for a short time. My pride and confidence swelled.

The next day, Jack and I took a tour of the Bell helicopter plant located a few miles away. I saw how well the chopper was built. I was impressed with how the workers treated us, once they knew Jack flew their product in combat. The tour guide was quick to express my brother's accomplishments as we continued our tour of the factory. Everyone was shaking Jack's hand. I came here impressed with the aircraft, but left much more impressed with my brother! We were given a flying demonstration of the new Cobra helicopter. I had not seen the aircraft before and was blown away by its style, power and agility. It was a weekend that I'll never forget!

The weeks in class went by swiftly. Denise and I enjoyed our first Christmas together away from home. I was now close to being a full-fledged jet engine mechanic in the United States Air Force. Soon, orders came down for our next duty assignment. I was going to Dyess AFB in Abilene, Texas. (I began to wonder if I was ever going to get out of Texas.) Bob, my "buddy," was not. So much for the "buddy system," I thought. He was sent to Norton AFB in California to work on T-29s. It would be years before I would see him again.

Upon graduation, we drove that little Mustang back up to Washington to return it to my brother. Somewhere in New Mexico, we backed into a fire hydrant and poked a hole in the back of Mick's pride and joy. It got worse.

Hundreds of miles later, in the mountains of Colorado around midnight, we crested a large peak and had just started down the other side when the lights went out! It was pitch-black, and we were traveling at fifty miles an hour! I still had power, but no lights at all, including brake lights to warn the semi truck that was now bearing down on us from behind! The truck roared past, swerving at the last minute to avoid us. He offered no assistance. I had no choice but to speed up to keep him in sight. I tried to use his taillights as navigational aids. We were now racing down an icy Colorado mountain in the dead of night with no lights to see or be seen by. I was able to use the semi's taillights for a few dangerous miles.

Finally, we came across a small gas station that thankfully was open at this late hour. We pulled over and I got out of the car. I was shaking. I soon discovered that the poke from the Mexican hydrant had pushed on the TV that I had packed in the trunk. It was resting nicely against a bundle of wires. The wires soon wore through and shorted out, causing the lights to go out. I taped the wires and replaced the fuse. We were back on the road in minutes. I was wide- awake!

We eventually reached Washington and the safety of home. I dreaded showing Mick his newly remodeled Mustang. To his credit, he was calm and very understanding. What a relief! We had a week or two of leave and I roamed around Bellevue in my crisp new uniform with one stripe and two ribbons (National Defense and Marksmanship). I was damn proud! The war was still going on, of course, and the peace marches were getting more out of hand each week. Being in uniform was not necessarily a good idea. At one restaurant, a fellow walked past me and simply whispered, "asshole." I was feeling patriotic at a time when it was dangerous to do so. This was my own hometown, and now I was made to feel unwelcome.

Before long, it was time to make the drive back to Texas. My brother, Jack, had taken a job flying Lear jets in Puerto Rico. He offered his clean '67 Chevy wagon at a bargain price to keep it in the family. I jumped at the deal. Denise drove the station wagon, while I drove my 1960 Corvette. We went hundreds of miles out of our way so I could avoid poor roads and protect the custom paint on my car. My younger brother, Maurie, rode along with us, alternating cars every few hours to keep us company. While riding with me, he would make up stories with sound effects on an old tape recorder. We soon discovered that a short burst with the microphone held outside the window, at seventy miles an hour, made great sounds of explosions. We took our stories to new heights. Sometimes I was laughing so hard I had tears in my eyes and had difficulty seeing the road. We spent hours this way, and Maurie unwittingly helped calm my nerves about my next duty assignment.

THREE

Dyess Air Force Base

A RRIVING IN ABILENE, WE FOUND A CUTE LITTLE apartment from a local newspaper ad. The studio type apartment was located above a two-car garage. It was small but inexpensive and smelled like maple syrup. We arrived on a Friday, so we spent the weekend discovering Abilene. Railroad tracks seemed to split the town in two. We spent a few hours driving around both sides. Denise joked about hoping our new home was on the *right* side of the tracks. Maurie seemed to be having fun and saying goodbye to him Sunday at Abilene's airport was difficult. I reported into the squadron the next day.

Dyess Air Force Base was named in honor of Lieutenant Colonel William Dyess, an outstanding hero of WW II. I was proud to be here, but I felt unsure about what lay ahead. Our little apartment, as it turned out, was about five miles away from the main gate of the air base.

After showing my orders to the Air Policeman at the main gate, I was provided with a map and directions to my new squadron. The smartly dressed Airman saluted as I sped away. The base itself was quite large and it took me awhile to find the right area. I was assigned to the 347th Tactical Airlift Squadron, one of two C-130 squadrons on base, under the 516th Tactical Airlift Wing. I found the squadron area, but there were no airplanes! I had just missed by a matter of weeks, the squadron going TDY (temporary duty) to Germany. The time was put to good use however, as I enrolled in the C-130E model familiarization course. The newer "E" model aircraft had improved avionics, larger fuel capacity and more powerful engines. By the time I had completed the month and a half training course, our airplanes were returning from overseas.

I met most of the people in the squadron and soon was assigned to an aircraft. I was one of three assistant crew chiefs on aircraft number 63-7805. Unlike the shiny chrome "A" model from tech school, the C-130s here were painted tan and green camouflage. The underside of the fuselage and wing area was painted white.

Soon I was standing alone for the first time in front of my aircraft as it started engines. I stood before the giant transport as the jet engines driving their huge four- bladed props grabbed at the air and roared. It was like controlled thunder! It was tremendous to stand there with all the noise and vibrations and *feel* the power. I was in absolute awe. Next, holding my arms high above my head, I marshaled the C-130 onto the taxiway and felt the warm exhaust from its engines as the pilot moved toward the runway. Wow!

Beside the two C-130 squadrons, Dyess AFB was home to a squadron of KC-135 tanker aircraft, a squadron of C-7 Caribou and a squadron of B-52 bombers. Security was very strict and we all wore special badges to have access to the flight line. The flight line itself was huge! It covered many acres and usually required a tug or a truck just to get around.

Each morning we would start the day by making FOD (Foreign Object Damage) sweeps. We would line up in a straight line among our aircraft and walk the flight line in search of any small objects that could be ingested into our engine intakes.

Soon I was in the swing of things, performing preflight and post-flight inspections of my aircraft. I learned to refuel with JP-4 jet fuel and liquid oxygen. Both were hairy procedures initially. The JP-4 was so volatile that with any hint of a spark I would go up in flames with my aircraft. The liquid oxygen was so cold that if I got any on my skin, it would shatter. We were shown back in tech-school how a banana dipped in liquid oxygen and dropped to the ground would smash into a thousand pieces. I remembered that lesson and always wore the protective apron and gloves. And, of course, I had not forgotten the Huey helicopter that went up in jet fueled flames.

It was not long before I got my first ride on my own aircraft. Our flight was a check ride locally, with a few touch-and-goes on the adjacent dirt strip next to the main runway. It was exciting, to say the least.

One afternoon during my preflight inspection, as I casually jumped from my right paratroop door to the ground, I felt a hard and quick tug from my left hand. I was in mid-air when my wedding ring snagged in the door track. Luck was on my side as it twisted in the track and broke free. I landed hard and down on one knee. I realized how close I had come to losing my finger! Immediately, I removed my ring and never again wore it around my aircraft. We had been taught by our tech school instructors not to wear jewelry on our jobs, but I was a proud newlywed. I learned a very valuable lesson that day, almost the hard way.

I started checking the schedules in squadron operations to see which aircraft were flying where. Mounted on one wall was a list of all of the squadrons' aircraft by tail number. Next to each aircraft were that month's scheduled missions. So, usually I would know early in the month where I would be flying to and for how long. The fellows working in Squadron Operations were a rare breed. They were enclosed in a darkened room, working on illuminated status boards. These boards showed the constantly changing status of all the squadrons' aircraft. It was a world apart from the flight line. Here it was dark and cool, while outside it was hot in the bright Texas sun.

I began to fly a few short trips to Oklahoma and other bases in Texas. Before long I was making one, two and three day trips all over the United States. We would RON or remain-over-night at the numerous Air Force bases throughout the country. I got along well with most of the flight crews and even got on a first name basis with some of the pilots.

One evening, I was in the cargo area of my plane, when a colonel stomped onboard and said, "Let's get this aircraft in the air, now!"

"Yes, sir!" I replied and promptly started removing the engine intake covers and "remove before flight" streamers. I had the ground power unit already plugged into the aircraft to give me electrical power, so I got on the headset outside and manned the fire bottle and got ready for engine start.

"Starting engine No. 3," said the colonel from the pilot's seat.

"You're cleared to start," I said and we did.

"Starting engine No. 2," the colonel said.

"Clear to start," I replied over the intercom.

"Airman, what is your name?" the colonel asked. Thinking he was impressed with my military bearing and starting procedures, I proudly said, "Airman Combs, sir."

"Airman Combs, would you come up here to the flight deck please?" he said. Puzzled, I headed into the aircraft and climbed the stairs to the flight deck. "Airman Combs, I have just stolen your aircraft," he announced. I'd been had. This had been a security test, and I failed. With a closer look at the colonel's (fake) security badge, I noted the signature plain as day. Mickey Mouse, it read. I felt like crawling into a hole. We shut down the two running engines and walked into operations where the story was told to my supervisors. I learned my lesson and never again allowed anyone on my aircraft without proper ID. In the Air Force, the crew chief owns the aircraft when it is on the ground. He has the authority to remove anyone not authorized on it regardless of rank. I would later invoke this privilege on more than one occasion, much to my satisfaction.

****

On one mission, we were scheduled to make a four-day trip to the East Coast. We started off by having a three-star general hop a ride with us to Eglin AFB in Florida. As I was getting the aircraft ready for take-off, the general's staff car pulled alongside. I came over in time to help carry in his golf clubs and bags. I secured them in the cargo area and went about my business. We started engines, pulled chocks and taxied out to the runway. I had by now learned the routine.

In the flight deck behind the pilot, copilot and flight engineer and next to the navigator's table, was a crew bunk. It was well established that the top bunk belonged to the crew chief while in flight. Once we were airborne, I came up to the flight deck from the cargo area and went on to pour a cup of coffee from the galley. The general asked if I wouldn't mind making him one as well. "Not at all, General," I replied. "In fact, I have a can of soup if you would like to share." He said he did, so I put it into the small micro-oven and heated it up to go with our coffee. The general and I sat on the lower crew bunk enjoying the hot meal and talking about the Air Force. He was a good guy it seemed, and when he asked if he could use the upper bunk, I replied, "Of course, sir." As he made himself comfortable, I jumped down from the flight deck and walked to the back of the cargo area of the aircraft. I stopped and chatted with the loadmaster. After a while, I just curled up on the red troop seat and slept.

Upon landing at Eglin AFB in Florida, I helped the general take his golf clubs and bags to the staff car that had just pulled up in front of our still running aircraft. Over the roar of our turboprop engines, the general thanked me for the soup and use of my bunk and stretched his hand out to shake mine. I shook his hand and he disappeared into the back of the staff car.

Back on board the aircraft, I hooked up to inter-phone. "Captain Brown-nose," the pilot, asked me why I did not salute the general. I told him the three-star offered his hand and I figured that was enough. "Captain Brown-nose" didn't agree and promised to write me up on report. Days later back at Dyess, I was called before the wing commander and asked my side of the story. He was satisfied with that. I saluted the commander and went back to work. That was the end of it. I wish I could remember who the three-star general was.

On a trip to Pope AFB in North Carolina, we participated in and passed our ORI (Operation Readiness Inspection). Having failed two before my arrival with the squadron, we were in a festive mood. The aircrews were staying in a motel off base, and we tore it up. Guys were drinking beer out of their combat boots and swimming in the motel pool at 3:00 in the morning. Early that morning, we had to fly back to Dyess. Everyone onboard clutched an airsickness bag in one hand or had one stashed strategically nearby. We looked and felt horrible...all of us from the pilot on down. I had never gotten airsick before, but this was the closest I ever came. I decided drinking and flying didn't mix.

I had taken the required test and passed for my next stripe. I was now an Airman First Class. Denise proudly removed my single stripes and replaced them with the two stripes of my new rank. We would make a few dollars more a month, and we would soon have more expenses. I felt especially proud to remove the single stripes I had earned from Basic Training.

****

Denise was pregnant! I'll always remember the joy when hearing the news as she and I embraced in the tiny kitchen of our apartment. I was on top of the world. Right away we started looking for a larger place. Our landlord lived in the main house next to our (his) garage apartment and mentioned in conversation one day that he owned a little two-bedroom trailer across town. The drive to base would be longer, but the added space and the rate was too good to pass up. The next afternoon, Denise and I took a ride over to look at the trailer. We checked everything inside and out and walked throughout the small trailer park. The park consisted of maybe eight or nine other mobile homes. A small breeze whistled through a strand of nearby trees as we stood trying to decide if we wanted this. My wife agreed, it seemed quiet and peaceful and we loved the inside of our trailer. With a hug we approved our next move. Two weeks later at the start of the new month, some of the guys from the squadron, including John Forsberg, showed up to help. They gave up their valuable weekend time just to help us move. We were making good friends.

The additional space was terrific and we came to love that little trailer with our soon-to-be-occupied nursery. Our Siamese cat loved it too as she was soon pregnant as well. Months later she gave birth to a single kitten. We didn't have the heart to separate the two, so we sort of kept the kitty. Occasionally in a casual way, we asked friends if anyone wanted a kitten. Soon it was apparent though, we had another member in our family. Cat and kitten were inseparable. They went everywhere and did everything together.

Early one morning as I was leaving for the base and an early take-off, I saw in my headlights our two cats across the street. Just as if they were rushing over to see me off, both mother and daughter came running across the street. Halfway across with no warning and no lights, a car came speeding past. The cat was fast enough to dart out of the way, but the kitten could not. I watched in horror as that tiny animal was devoured by the car's right-front tire. I yelled to Denise to grab a towel and come quickly. I got out of the car and ran to the curb. The speeding car was gone; it didn't even slowdown. I found our little kitty still alive and bleeding. Denise arrived with a towel and I gently picked up our dying kitten. We drove to the vet's office about a mile away. The doc tried for some time to save her but without success. He suggested we put her out of her obvious misery. Denise and I held and stroked the kitten while the doctor injected her. Her howls grew weaker and soon stopped. We drove back to the trailer in tears. We were both a mess. I called the squadron and they offered the day off. We spent the day comforting not only one another, but also our poor Siamese cat. Our home was never the same after that.

Denise and I started looking for another place. Eventually we found a little two-bedroom house with a crooked detached garage. The small house was located on the other side of town. We now lived on Mulberry Street. It was a quiet street and we tried to keep the cat in the house as much as possible. Denise and I hoped this side of the tracks would be luckier.

I had many friends by now but palled around mostly with John Forsberg. John, of course, was in my class at Sheppard AFB, graduating at the same time. The sandy-haired A1C was single and from Connecticut. After tech school John flew home and weeks later drove his car back down to Texas. He was a great guy, and we often tooled around base in my Corvette or his red Willy's Jeep. John and I had hit it off right away at Technical School, and it was nice to have a friend or familiar face in new surroundings.

With the additional stripe sewn on, I now tested for a Secret clearance and took my flight physical. The physical was like any other I had experienced except, this time they took footprints as well as fingerprints. The footprints, we were told, were for identification in case of a crash or shoot down. Sometimes the only part left to identify is what's laced up inside your flight boots. We were also told to be sure our personal things were in order. We filled out forms on life insurance and wills, etc. It was a sobering thought.

One night on swing shift, John and I left the flight line and drove up to the little snack bar by the B-52 squadron. It was one of those buffet style places where you dispense your own soft drinks or milkshakes. I chose a chocolate shake, gripped a cup and went on to fill it. However when I nearly reached the top, the machine would not shut off. I frantically grabbed other cups to fill and John shouted for the cook to come out front. He must have been out back grabbing a smoke, because no one came around. We skipped the shake and ran out the door with the shake machine still pouring out chocolate ice cream everywhere! I would like to have seen the look on the cook's face when he returned.

FOUR

First Rotation

WE WERE GOING TDY TO ENGLAND! The squadron's rotation that I had missed months before was upon us again. This time, I would participate. I was issued cold weather gear and a flight suit and quickly sewed on the squadron and command patches. The whole Tactical Wing would go. The air and ground crews along with support personnel from both C-130 squadrons made ready. Over thirty of our squadrons' aircraft would make the trip across the Atlantic.

Two of our C-130s left one day ahead of the rest of us and were going to Goose Bay, Labrador for the first leg of the trip. I flew out the next day with my cargo bay full of support equipment strapped down on pallets. We headed north and arrived well after dark. I can assure you, the bright approach lights of Goose Bay airfield were a welcome to all of us in the flight deck that night. For the longest time, the sky outside had been pitch black! It seemed as if we had left civilization behind hours ago. This was a remote place. Instead of having to stay back and post-flight my aircraft, we were allowed to grab a meal and bed down for the night. The ground crews who flew in ahead of us would be there to do maintenance on the squadron's aircraft as we all came through the area.

The barracks they put us in were right next to the WAF's barracks (Women of the Air Force). We stayed up most of the night peeking through the blinds. We could see a number of ladies in a wide variety of undress. Most it seemed, knew we were watching and made a game out of it. We enjoyed the show. Besides, there was little else to do up here in remote Labrador.

The next morning during our preflight, a crew chief from another C-130 stopped by to ask a "small" favor. Seems his aircraft required a prop change. My crew chief offered to stay behind to help his friend. I took over as acting crew chief on aircraft 805. I confidently finished my preflight inspection and made ready for the long flight. Shortly after preflight, we were in the air heading east across the Atlantic Ocean. I roamed throughout the aircraft during flight. Most often I was hooked up to the aircraft's intercom system. Various stations throughout the C-130 were equipped with plug-ins for intercom. I kept a fairly long cord with me and this allowed me to venture throughout the entire plane from nose to tail and always connected. Just keeping the headphones on and over my ears helped to diminish the noise whether I was plugged in or not.

Many hours later, we landed briefly somewhere in Ireland. Everything it seemed was bathed in green. While I was waiting for the fuel truck to arrive, I noticed the breathtaking beauty of the nearby countryside. The entire area had that old country charm. With the refueling complete, we took off again. Now we were flying directly to Mildenhall AB in England.

"RAF Mildenhall is known as the gateway to the United Kingdom. It's located in Suffolk County," announced the pilot over the intercom. "RAF bombers left Mildenhall field only hours after England declared war on Germany. It was 1939. They were sent after German battleships. In a way, England's' response to Hitler started right down there," said the captain, pointing out the side glass window.

"You guys need to spend some time looking around," added the copilot, as he reached forward to lower the landing gear. "The base is very interesting, especially if you like history."

I sat down on the crew bunk and strapped in for landing. The gear locked down with a thud, precisely at the moment my belt clicked into place. It made me feel strangely connected. The crew started our final approach checklist as I sat back on the lower bunk. My mind was racing with the possibilities of what lay ahead. I was eager and in charge of my airplane for the first time. It felt good.

Our crew was the first to arrive in England. We touched down gently on the Mildenhall runway. The pilot reversed our engines rapidly to come to a quick stop. We turned onto a taxiway and saw a blue Air Force pickup truck racing out to meet us. "You've got to look good for the locals," said the pilot about his landing.

We lumbered behind the "follow-me" truck as it delivered us to the assigned area of the flight line. The spot he gave us was superb. We were parked in close and directly in front of operations. Once everyone was off the aircraft, I started my post-flight inspection. I called for a fuel truck and an oxygen cart when the line truck stopped by. The driver asked where we had come from. I told him we were the 347th from Dyess, Texas. As he started another question, the roar of a C-130 reversing its props on landing drowned out his voice. Ignoring the question for a moment, I turned to see one of our squadron's aircraft racing past on the runway. The giant DZ on the tail was a clue that the C-130 was one of ours. As it got closer, I could make out the serial number. This C-130 was number 816, John Forsberg's airplane. I turned back to the driver in the blue Air Force truck as he made more calls on his radio. The driver said local ground crews are on their way to refuel and post-flight for us. This was great! We were free to grab some chow and find a bed. However, I never made it that far.

In the chow hall, our squadron commander came up to me and asked me where my crew chief was. I explained that he had remained behind at Goose Bay to help someone and that I was acting crew chief. The commander told us to finish our chow and head back to the flight line. Something had come up. We rifled down some food and headed for the flight line. I got back to my aircraft within minutes. The commander had already arrived and was now talking to some of the crew. Right away I was told by the commander to get ready for take-off.

"Sir, where are we going?" I asked. A number of crewmembers were now gathering under the left wing of my aircraft as the commander turned and said softly, "I can't tell you." Pausing for a moment the colonel scratched at his chin. He needed a shave. I thought he was going to change his mind, but instead he turned to me and simply asked, "Where are your bags?" "Sir, they were off-loaded and taken to the barracks, but we don't know where the barracks are yet," I told him. "I'll take care of your bags," he announced. With a salute he turned and walked away shouting over his shoulder to all of us, "You'll likely be back later today."

The only C-130s ready to fly were 805 and 816. John Forsberg's crew chief was also still in Goose Bay helping the others. This meant we were both "acting" crew chiefs.

Within a half hour we were airborne and heading south. As I stood in the flight deck, the navigator ripped open a sealed envelope and read it over the intercom to the rest of us. Terrorists had hijacked a commercial airliner and flown it to the desert somewhere in the Middle East. We were headed for Incirlik Air Base in Turkey and were to stand by for further instructions.

It was late by the time we cruised high over Turkish air space. I could see lights and traffic down below. From my position it looked like any small city or town in the U.S. "I sure hope we have time to visit the compound," said the flight engineer. "What's the compound?" I asked. The engineer explained that under Turkish law, if a man were convicted of a crime, his wife, sister or mother would serve his sentence, prostituting her in the compound. This way, the man was still available to work at his job, thereby keeping the economy alive. I doubted his story, but then again he had been here before.

We touched down at Incirlik Air Base, taxied to a hardstand and shut down the engines. The pilots, navigator, engineer and loadmaster all went into debrief, leaving me alone to post-flight my aircraft. The pilot had written up a few discrepancies, so I set about the task of getting them fixed.

A young American dressed in jeans and a plaid shirt, drove up in the line truck and said something about being off duty before quickly offering to tow a power unit over to me. As he dropped it off next to my airplane, I waved casually and yelled, "Hey, thanks, man!" John Forsberg's C-130 was parked next to mine, and he was also working on his aircraft now. By the time we had both finished, it was very early in the morning.

After locking down our planes, we hitched a ride to base operations. From there, we caught a ride to the transient barracks. John and I groped our way down the dark aisle looking for available beds. Finally way at the back, we found a couple of empty cots. John and I just dropped down, removed our boots and slept in our flight-suits. The whole barracks woke up at 6:00 a.m. and there was enough noise to keep us awake. We got up, showered, put on our same clothes and headed back to the flight line.

I started to check over my aircraft and noticed right away, by walking around under the wings, the shade provided strong relief from the rising heat of the Turkish sun. I grabbed the ground power unit for electrical power. Now with power switched on at the GPU, I climbed the stairs to the flight deck and moved the switches on the overhead panel to gain power. I started some coffee brewing in the galley and began my pre-flight inspection.

It was cooler inside my main landing gear wheel-wells. I could always "feel the weight" of my aircraft bearing down on me when I was in there. (Only another C-130 crew chief will know how this feels.) The smell of rubber and hydraulic fluid was strong. I proceeded to check the area with my flashlight. I was looking for anything out of the ordinary. Thankfully, everything checked out: no hydraulic leaks, the brake pads looked fine and still good tread on the tires. No cuts. I moved to the nose gear and jumped inside. This wheel-well was different. It was lighter and roomier. I sometimes felt like I was sitting in the bow of a ship!

I continued my preflight inspection and waited for the flight crew. My inspections would take me under, in and on top of my aircraft. As always, I used my checklist. This method would provide an orderly "tour" of the airplane. As I was finishing my inspection, the flight engineer came out to the aircraft and said we were to attend a meeting at Base Operations.

I closed up my aircraft and cut the power. John Forsberg was a wingtip away doing the same thing. Once finished we walked to base operations together. Within minutes, we began filing into a room dominated by a long teak or rosewood table. The crews from both aircraft were present. Scattered about the table were pots of coffee and numerous cups, plus six or seven walkie-talkie radios. I grabbed an early seat close to the door.

Across the room and at the far end of the table, sat the pilot of my aircraft; he was talking on the phone. When he hung up, he said that was the Pentagon on the line and our instructions were to remain here on a one-hour alert. That meant at any given time day or night, we would have to be in the air within one hour of notification. Two more C-130s from our sister squadron (the 348th) at Dyess were en-route. They had been diverted from our base in England just as we had.

"The terrorist group is the Popular Front for the Liberation of Palestine," said the pilot. "Over the past few days, the PFLP has hijacked a Swissair DC-9, a TWA Boeing 707 and a Pan Am 747. The aircraft are on the ground in Jordan." he continued, "The passengers and crews are being held somewhere outside of Amman. In case you haven't read a newspaper lately, I'll fill you in. Jordan is right in the middle of a civil war! These PFLP guys are armed and roaming the streets like they owned them." The pilot took a long drink from his coffee cup and continued. "And, they have already blown up two of the airliners and most likely will destroy the third."

"What's our mission, Captain?" asked one of the navigators. "Wait, it gets worse," he answered. "The Syrians have launched an attack from the north. They have tanks and artillery and are capable of shooting us down."

Then there was a knock on the door, and the pilot buzzed the new arrival in with a button mounted next to his phone. The young American was the same fellow who helped me find a ground power unit for my airplane the night before. Only then, he was wearing civilian clothes and I figured by his age, he was an Airman first class or sergeant. Now, he glides into the room in his dress blues and he's sportin' no fewer than *seven* stripes!

"They promote 'em often in these remote areas," remarked the man next to me, as the young Senior Master Sergeant approached the pilot. He spoke into the pilot's ear briefly while handing him a sealed envelope. Once the young sergeant left the room, we turned our attention back to the captain. Looking up from a sheet of paper he said flatly, "Another airliner has been hijacked. This one is a VC-10 out of Bahrain." The pilot took another long drag from his coffee cup and continued. "The United States and the Soviet Union are working together to peacefully resolve this. Our mission will be humanitarian, focused on getting as many people to safety as we can. We need to stay close and in touch with each other. We could launch at any time."

The pilot rose from his chair and turned to me, "Chief, you and I need to stay close to each other. Keep your radio nearby and turned on." I pushed back my chair and walked to the far end of the table. The pilot handed me a radio from the pile. "Yes sir, I'm ready and so is eight-oh-five," I boasted.

The air base also provided us with four Econoline trucks for our use. John Forsberg and I grabbed one and headed to the chow hall. After a questionable powdered egg breakfast, we drove around awhile to check the layout of the base. In the process, we located a vacant barracks and discovered it was available to us. At least if we had to spend another night here, we would be much more comfortable. The rooms had two beds each and shared a common bathroom with an adjoining room. We explored a little more of the base then went back to the flight line and hung around our aircraft.

The other two C-130s arrived around mid afternoon and we helped the other crew chiefs post-flight their aircraft. Another meeting was held in the base operations conference room and my pilot (who seemed to be in charge) received more calls from the State Department and the Pentagon. It was apparent by now that we would be here at least a day or two more, so a few of us went to the Base Exchange and bought some basic toiletries. I purchased three pairs of underwear.

Each day for the next four or five days, nothing changed. We had our "Pentagon" meetings each morning and remained ready on one-hour alert. It was rumored among my friends that one of the newly arriving crew chiefs from the 348th was from Seattle, Washington.

The next morning while standing in the crew entrance door of my C-130, I noticed a blond, well-built man walking over. He introduced himself as he stuck out his right hand. Grabbing my hand firmly in his he announced, "Hi, I'm John Rhett from Seattle." He had bright eyes and a ready smile. Yes, he was actually from West Seattle, he explained. John, who was an Airman 1st class as well, had me relaxed and laughing almost immediately. We talked about familiar turf back home and what schools we'd gone to. It felt good to have a familiar friend, although it felt strange to meet one so far away from home. I introduced John Rhett to John Forsberg later that morning. All three of us hit it off immediately. Little did we know this was only the beginning of many adventures for the three of us.

Days were spent around our aircraft in constant preparation. I wanted to be sure my one-thirty was ready to go. I double-checked everything. At night, we hung around our room and played poker. The base had a club for officers but not much for the enlisted men. Air Police guarded our aircraft now, around the clock.

One evening, a couple of officers from my aircrew came by our room and invited us to the officers' club. "But we can't go in there," I protested. With a wink and a grin, the pilot gave me his captain bars and I put them on my flight suit, which normally had no rank insignia anyway. I was now Captain Combs! "This way, we're all together if we get the call," remarked the pilot. John Forsberg and John Rhett were also "promoted" on the spot. The officers were well known already at the club so the doorman wouldn't question their missing rank insignia. That was the idea, and it worked perfectly. We all laughed and patted ourselves on the back as we sauntered into the air-conditioned club acting as officer buddies. Hey this feels cool, I thought to myself.

So we enjoyed a few nights playing officers and playing poker. I remember noticing the first night in the O'club behind the bar, a picture of U-2 pilot Francis Gary Powers. There were a few pictures of various U-2s in flight as well.

"This is where he launched from," commented the copilot sitting next to me. "Some say it was the flight that changed the world."

"We sure got caught with our flight suits down that time," joked the navigator. "It all started right here at Incirlik, then over to Peshawar, Afghanistan, and on up to the Soviet Union," added one of the local officers, as he raised the table two more dollars.

Next to the U-2 pictures were a few of an A-model C-130. I asked the navigator sitting to my right about the significance of the C-130 in the photos. "That's 60528," he said. "About twelve years ago, on September 2, 1958, the C-130 was assigned, like we are now, TDY to Incirlik." Folding his cards and lighting a cigarette he continued with his story. "The aircraft flew into Soviet-Armenian airspace and they were shot down by MIG-17s...seventeen men and one American military plane gone. They were on an ELINT [Electronic Intelligence] mission eavesdropping on the Soviets and accidentally flew off course." The nav took another long drag from his cigarette and remarked slowly, "This is a dangerous area to be flying around."

I was blown away. This was the first I had ever heard of a C-130 being shot down. It just never occurred to me that this type of airplane would somehow become a target in the Cold War. It was a long time ago, but the situation around us remained the same. Strict flight corridors were assigned and were to be adhered to with grave consequences for mistakes. Our mission suddenly became in my mind, even more perilous. That someone would shoot down an unarmed transport plane seemed hard to believe, even if it was on a spy mission. I was fast learning the realities of world geo-politics. The officers club here at Incirlik had become a sort of shrine to the previous flight-crews stationed here. I secretly hoped my C-130 would not appear on the wall for some future poker game conversation.

Understandably, I was having a hard time keeping up with my meager Airman's earnings. So were John Forsberg and John Rhett. By the third night of impersonating officers, we bowed out and stayed behind in our barracks. I was also having a hard time staying away from the latrine. All of us had the "Turkey trots." No matter what I ate, it went through me with a vengeance.

One evening, the three of us went to the base community club. We could get a meal there, do some letter writing or read a book. This particular night, they had a live band playing. Some American GIs who were unlucky enough to be stationed there, had put together a little group to entertain themselves and the troops. John Forsberg knew I played drums from our conversations back at Dyess, so he "volunteered" me to sit-in on a song. I did reluctantly and we played "Hey Jude" by the Beatles. Not exactly a drummer's delight, but I had a good time.

****

Our mail was late getting to us having been routed first from the U.S. to Mildenhall, then to our remote base in Turkey. We looked forward each day to mail-call as it became our only link to the outside world and our families back home. One evening I received a letter from my first cousin, Gerry Watson. He was in the Army. While I was away from home with the Air Force, cousin Gerry had the draft board breathing down his neck. He chose the Army with the idea of two years active then a reserve commitment after that. The letter was postmarked from Fort Benning, Georgia. He had just finished Basic Training at Fort Ord, California, and was now going to jump school. My cousin and boyhood friend had already made a few static-line jumps from C-130s. I wondered if our paths would cross in the near future with Gerry jumping from my bird. I worried about him though, as Vietnam was most probably in his future as well. Enclosed in his letter was a photo showing him in full combat gear standing outside his barracks, smiling.

****

By now we had Pentagon meetings at base operations twice each day. During one morning briefing we were told that we would be going into Jordan to rescue some of the passengers from the hijacked planes. It was decided we should paint red crosses on each of our C-130s. This was an attempt to look humanitarian and not like a commando raid. We hoped the red crosses would prevent them from opening up on us. That was the idea anyway. So, out we went to our parked aircraft. Right away I opened all the doors to let the hot air out. It must have been over 120 degrees inside my cargo bay!

With the use of a cherry picker (a large crane) and a man from the base paint shop, I was hoisted to the vertical stabilizer of my aircraft. We taped off then painted a giant white square in the center. Within this huge square, we then painted a cross in red. We did this on each side of the tail and under both wings. Forsberg and Rhett also had red crosses painted on their C-130s. It was late at night by the time all four aircraft had Red Cross markings. As crew chiefs we often pitched in to help each other with our duties. That way we shared the work and could share the fun as well. So far though, we were not having a whole lot of fun. Painting the red crosses on the aircraft was to be a difficult do-it-yourself job in the hot Turkish sun.

During one of our base operations meetings, we got word that the terrorists had blown up the last airplane in the desert outside of Amman. The passengers were being held hostage at undisclosed locations. Around-the-clock negotiations were being conducted in secret. This was being done behind the scenes at the highest levels to secure the release of the hostages. Meanwhile, we waited.

We soon realized in this hot, humid weather, that we had to run our engines periodically. I stood ground fire-watch while Forsberg ran up his engines and he did the same for me. Neither one of us were formally authorized to do this. But here in Turkey, who would know? Since no one questioned our actions and because we did know what we were doing, we ran our engines each day. By now I had a healthy respect for my airplane and enjoyed having more power to exercise around it. However, we were all itching to get into the air again or at least away from Turkey.

Each evening, a man would emerge from a small opening near the top of a nearby tower. He would sing a beautiful Turkish song. It made me realize how far away from home I was. Turkey was in a way, exotic and mystical. I'm sure the music he sang was religious and held great meaning, but to me it was simply a beautiful way to usher in the night. I watched over my C-130 knowing it could be needed at anytime. I wanted to be ready.

****

We had been on constant one-hour alert status for three weeks. Occasionally, we had false alarms, causing us to tear down the street at breakneck speed to get to the flight line, only to be told that the situation had changed and to "go back to what you were doing." This happened once at three in the morning when I heard a loud squawk and then a tired, "Chief, are you there? Come in, Chief!" I had the radio turned on and lying next to my head and pillow. I nearly jumped at the suddenness of the pilot's radio call. The volume must have been on high. I answered his call and switched on the light. We dressed and ran out the door. When we got to our airplanes no one else had arrived yet, so each of us started to pull intake covers and streamers from our engines. I put power to my C-130 right away so I would have light to start my preflight. About twenty minutes later, one of the navigators came out to inform us that we were to stand down. Damn!

****

One morning my aircraft was given a special mission to a remote base in northern Turkey. The aircrew came out and said "let's launch." While we started our preflight together, the pilot mentioned we were going north for a special reason. He would like to have me along in case we broke down. He promised it would not be more than a few hours. Weeks of "turkey trots" were taking their toll on me, and I was getting weak. Once airborne, I curled up on my bunk in the flight deck and fell fast asleep to the constant RPMs of our turboprops.

I awoke with a start! I had the clearest feeling of dread and gloom and felt oddly perplexed. All was completely quiet. I looked out the flight deck windows and saw that we were parked on the ground in a deserted area. I jumped down from my bunk and came down the stairs to the cargo compartment. To my surprise I had slept through the landing and at least one major event onboard. Strapped down in the center of the cargo compartment was a bright silver casket! No wonder I awoke and felt strange. I was alone in my airplane with a dead person. I opened the crew entrance door and wandered over to the only building standing nearby. This place was desolate.

I had to use the toilet again, but to my surprise there was none! Instead of toilets, these folks simply had a hole in the ground and little footpads on each side. I was in no position to wait, so I planted by feet and did my business. Next surprise was no toilet paper. I was expected to wipe with my hands then wash my hands in the sink. Was this all a dream? Now I could have used the "honey bucket" in my cargo compartment, but if I did, I was the one who would have to clean it. Plus there was a casket in my plane. I just didn't feel right about doing my business next to it.

Outside, I located my crew as they gathered together not far away. They were gazing in the direction of Russia and the Black Sea. The area we were in was called Samsun. After a short geography lesson, we headed back to the aircraft and I jumped on interphone. "Pilot, you're clear to start number three," I said. We went through engine start up and I coiled up the interphone cord as I climbed aboard my C-130. Once we were back in the air, the pilot explained to me that our cargo was an Air Force sergeant. He had been positioned up here at a remote VHF intercept station and had died, apparently of a heart attack. Ours was the first leg of a long trip home for the deceased Airman.

Back at Incirlik, things were starting to get out of hand. We were told that we would be rescuing people in need of medical attention, so we should remove the troop seats and the dual rails (used for rolling cargo in and out) and install the litters. I did this in the hot sweltering Turkish sun, only to be told the very next day, to take down the litters and put up the troop seats. I toiled again in the hot sun, stopping occasionally to run across the tarmac to the nearest outhouse. Once, I no sooner got back to my airplane than I had to spin around and run back to the outhouse. This was maddening!

****

John Forsberg, John Rhett and I were enjoying lunch one day in the cafeteria, when a beautiful blonde walked in the door. She moved over to the sales counter and brought back a cup and a napkin, then sat down at a table near us. Honestly, she looked like a model or a centerfold. She positioned herself facing us and right away gave us a smile. We acted cool and casual while we decided what our next move should be. All she had was a cup of coffee and no companion. Her table had four chairs and she occupied one of them. So we agreed, we would get up at the same time and simply walk over and sit down. The idea was each one of us would take a chair... yeah, safety in numbers.

After a few more looks and glances, the three of us stood up together pushing our chairs back with a collective screech. I looked at John Rhett on my left and Forsberg on my right. We nodded in agreement and proudly walked up to the blonde's table and sat down...well almost. As I pulled my chair in behind me, I looked her in the eyes and said, "Hi." At precisely that moment, I noticed my two "friends" waving to me from beyond. They had tricked me and actually had no intention of sitting at the woman's table at all. They had just walked on past! I was caught off guard for a moment and I think she knew what had just happened.

Yes, she was an American but not a WAF. She had flown in recently from the States and was waiting for her husband. "He's an F-4 pilot," she said proudly. Oops, no wonder no one else approached her! I told her only that I was on TDY from the States and missing home.

Her long wavy hair kept getting in her face as we talked. She would gently brush it aside with a slender hand as she spoke, whispered actually, in the sexiest voice I had heard in a long time! It was a pleasure just to watch her move and talk. She seemed starved for attention, so we sat and chatted awhile. Just long enough to get back at my friends, but not long enough to push my luck. I kept glancing at the door expecting a "phantom." Later, as we sat around in our room, I told my friends that she was a *Playboy* playmate on a USO tour. And, I added, she made a promise to send me a special autographed photo of herself. Served 'em right.

****

All of us were getting antsy by now, as we were approaching the fourth week in Turkey. One night I was driving the little Econoline truck around the base and was wondering why I didn't have as much power as before. I looked to my right in the dark cab and saw Rhett smiling broadly. I knew something was up because he looked so guilty. What was burning anyway? It turned out John Rhett had discreetly pulled the emergency brake handle, until the back tires locked up. He had covered up the noise of the screeching tires with the radio and his boisterous laughter. We had been driving around with semi-locked wheels and trailing smoke all the way. What a sight!

****

I was ordered again to take down the troop seats in my aircraft and install the litters. Sure enough having done this, I was told to take down the litters and put in the troop seats. At least the constant rotation of the seats and litters interrupted the monotony.

"We're going down to the compound," Forsberg said one afternoon. "Do you want to join us?"

"But we can't leave the base," I said.

"Who's going to know?" he asked. John had a point. We had been here almost a month and had not left the base, except for my only flight north. A flight engineer had given us directions to the compound and admitted he had been there once already this trip. "Okay," I said, "let's go!" The three of us grabbed a taxi and a two-way radio and away we went.

We roamed the dirty streets of Adana, Turkey, and were constantly pestered by shoeshine boys and kids offering tours or trinkets. Eventually we found our way to the compound's main gate. The armed guard looked at us suspiciously and frisked us for guns or knives. He looked suspiciously at our radio but let us pass. We entered the L-shaped street and started our tour. The area looked like a little village shopping district with cute window dressings. Only what were on display in the windows were definitely not mannequins. Each shop had a number of women sitting in chairs in the windows and they would smile or wink as we passed by. Some were very old and some looked too young to be here. At the end of the short block, the street made a ninety-degree turn to the right, then went for another half block and ended with a brick wall.

We strolled down one side and were just heading back up the other, when a very attractive lady in her twenties came out to see us. As the four of us stood there on the sidewalk, she picked me and took my hand pulling me towards the door, apparently to lead me upstairs. Not so fast!

I wasn't so sure about this, so I withdrew my hand and stood at the end of the tall curb. The attractive brunette must have thought I didn't like her. She took offense to my hesitation and before I knew it, she rushed at me with both arms outstretched shoving me off the curb and into a puddle of water. I stumbled and crashed down onto my back in the dirty, smelly liquid while she laughed and mocked me. Other ladies nearby saw this and joined in laughing, pointing and howling loudly. I was humiliated and told my pals I was ready to leave. They talked briefly with the black-haired beauty that had pushed me. At first I thought they were going to grab her and do to her what she had done to me. Prompted by the shouts and noise echoing here in the street, two armed "guards" suddenly made an appearance off to our left. I would have appreciated the gesture from my friends of course, but we were in a potentially dangerous situation here. My friends turned to the brunette and tried to explain my actions with words and gestures, but she spoke no English. Finally we agreed to just head back to the base. As we walked past the two guards, I prayed they were not going to stop us and start a hassle of some kind. We were not supposed to be there in the first place and getting arrested was out of the question. We just acted West Coast casual, talking and laughing our way right past the guards and out the front gate. Whew!

We found a taxi and were driven the few miles back to Incirlik. Along the way, we came across a caravan of gypsies on the right side of the road. The entire caravan looked as if they were from a Hollywood picture. They rode in old style covered wagons pulled by oxen. Some folks were walking along side the wagons as well. The taxi driver seemed intent on keeping his speed up so we roared past the block long caravan in seconds. But I'll always remember some of those gypsy faces. Once back on base, we discovered that no one had missed us. However, I decided I had seen quite enough of Adana.

The next morning we were gathered in the office for another State Department and Pentagon meeting. "A tentative cease-fire has been agreed to," the captain explained. "Let's hope they all agree not to fire on the red crosses."

"Hell we've probably just made it easier for their gunners to find us!

X marks the spot!" joked one of the loadmasters. No one laughed. We were more than ready to go. We were directed to wear our flight suits inside out so as not to show rank or any military insignia. Also, we were given white armbands with red crosses on them to wear on our left sleeves. It looked as if today or tomorrow would finally be the day.

Hours later, my two-way radio crackled to life. "Chief, it's a go, meet at the aircraft." We grabbed our gear and drove out to the flight line. I brought my camera as well.

At my aircraft I immediately began removing intake covers and ground streamers to get ready for engine start-up. We had made sure our batteries were charged also, just in case we had to shut down when we landed. Wherever we were going, we doubted they would have ground power units for our use.

I was on headphones and standing in front of my aircraft as we began engine start. Three of the four C-130s would go as directed, with the fourth staying behind as a backup. John Forsberg and John Rhett were going along with their respective aircrews as well.

We were airborne in a matter of minutes and headed south. The copilot got out of his seat and went to the cargo area and returned with an armful of pistol belts. I was given a .38-caliber pistol in a black holster. I casually strapped it on around my waist. I began to realize how serious this actually was. Everyone was upbeat and "business as usual"—at least on the outside. I had no doubts about our capabilities. Everyone knew his task and we were ready to get the job done. We had been waiting for this moment for many weeks.

Serious as it was, we still found time to laugh. We were wearing our flight suits inside out, with our armbands tied on one sleeve, carrying a pistol. We looked silly. Most of us agreed it was unusual, and we teased each other. Quickly changing the mood, the pilot came on the interphone and informed us that we were heading into Amman, Jordan. The civilians from one of the hijacked airliners had been taken to the airport in Amman, and we were to pick them up and fly them to Turkey. "One of our additional concerns," explained the pilot, "is the possibility that one or more of the hijackers will infiltrate the group and might pull the pin on a grenade on the ground or once we're airborne again. Blowing up an American military plane would be a bonus for their political cause."

As we circled the airstrip in Amman, we could see tanks and gun emplacements everywhere. Our three camouflaged C-130s with red cross markings, touched down on the rough strip, one after the other. I noticed as we came to a taxiing speed, that the barrels of the tanks and guns along both sides of the landing strip were aimed at us!

We moved over to the terminal area, and I stored my camera away after taking a few shots of the surrounding tanks. As we came to a stop, the loadmaster in the back started opening the rear cargo door and ramp. I came back to his station in the rear of the aircraft and surveyed the scene. There spread out before us, was the large group of hostages with their belongings. We kept engines running as the loadmaster and I started to let some of the people come aboard. We only allowed women and children to line up first. We searched each one before allowing them on the aircraft ramp. The copilot soon joined us. We checked baskets and bags. I was particularly wary of the men and expected one to pull a gun or grenade at any moment. However, all the hostages were very quiet and orderly, which to me was spooky. I kept watching their eyes for any sign of trouble. Soon the loadmaster was raising the ramp and we began to move among the hostages helping them get situated safely in the troop seats.

We had about 100 people—men women and children—all crowded aboard along with their belongings, and soon we were taxiing away from the terminal. Looking out the porthole, I could see the other two C-130s were doing the same thing. As we rumbled toward the end of the runway, I noticed the turrets on the tanks were slowly moving as they followed our progress. The turrets were aimed low and directly at us! I grabbed my camera and snapped a few more pictures through the small porthole window. I expected any one of the tanks to start firing at us as we taxied by. Like ducks in a gallery, I thought. We were in a small valley with renegade tanks and rocket propelled grenade launchers on *both* sides of us! I'm sure I was holding my breath as we moved from the taxiway to the end of the runway. Wasting no time, the pilot brought our engines to full throttle and released the brakes. The C-130 practically jumped into the air! We were not out of the woods yet, but I was feeling better as we flew higher.

Before long, all three of our C-130s were in the air and heading back to Turkey. I roamed the aisles in the cargo area, still concerned about a grenade attack. Most of the people reached out and patted my hand in thanks for their rescue. Ten minutes into our flight, I walked up the ladder to the flight deck and looked outside. I saw numerous tanks roaming the desert below us. I watched from the flight deck for a while, expecting to see shells bursting all around us. Later, I kept the loadmaster company as we both looked over our passengers. It wasn't long before we landed back at Incirlik and the civilians reached out to us again, touching our hands as they filed off the cargo ramp. They were put on blue Air Force buses and whisked away. We were told our mission was over and we could head home.

We were in no mood to hang around, so we quickly drove back to our barracks in our little Econoline truck and grabbed our things. Then we headed back to our aircraft. "Engine number three is clear to start," I said over interphone. "Starting number three," replied the pilot. "Let's get the hell out of here," someone said on interphone. No argument from me!

We had by now given our weapons back and turned our flight suits back around. We stashed our Red Cross armbands into our pockets and, except for the giant red crosses on my airplane, appeared "normal" again. It was a long flight back to England and most of us on the crew rehashed the day's events. The aircrew said I had performed an excellent job and should be proud. I was.

We had been away from the rest of our squadron for over a month. When we finally touched down back at Mildenhall, it was like joining a football game at halftime. Everyone there was settled in comfortably. They had been flying missions in support of NATO all over Europe and by now, knew all the hot spots locally around the air base.

Our squadron commander met us at the airplane and shook our hands. Other crew chiefs gathered around offering backslaps and handshakes. Right away they started asking us about our mission. Our four Hercules with the giant red crosses had attracted a lot of attention. My crew chief came up and shook his head in disbelief. He had not seen his airplane in over a month and, like a mother to a child, started looking it over from top to bottom. The chief had been assigned as a "floater" among the squadron's aircraft as he awaited my arrival. We had to go into a top secret debrief, so I left him with his baby (somewhat reluctantly, as it now felt like my airplane). I said I would tell him all about it later.

We were debriefed on the mission and cautioned about discussing certain parts of the events with anyone. We were given directions to the barracks. Our baggage, we were told had been stored in some lockers near the flight line. We immediately retrieved them. I had not seen my bag since leaving the U.S. over a month ago. I couldn't even remember what I had packed inside. Every item was a discovery. We were assigned rooms in a new three-story brick building across the street. I couldn't wait to get out of my flight suit, take a shower and get into some fresh clothes.

We were given a few days off, and I used that time to catch up on events in England. That first night, we went to a popular pub called The Bird-In-Hand. We drank English beer and listened to loud rock music from the jukebox. Someone in the pub must have loved the song "All Right Now" by Free, as it was played over and over. I reveled in the loud music. Anyone who has flown through Mildenhall knows The Bird-In-Hand. It was amazing to be sitting there sipping a pint in an old English pub, when only hours earlier we had been facing tanks and anti-aircraft guns. It was surreal, actually.

Meanwhile, in England some of the single guys in our squadron already had attracted girlfriends! Some, on occasion, had taken them out to their C-130s late at night for a most unauthorized "tour" of the airplane. The tour was usually confined to the flight deck bunks. I used the down time to get my pictures developed and write some letters to family. Two days later when I retrieved my pictures, I found they had been blanked out! The earlier pictures were fine, but those showing Amman and the tanks were blank. Censored!

It wasn't long before I was in the swing of things back in England. Each morning we would rise and shower. Once dressed, we'd walk to

Mickey's Tea Bar on the corner and have a "spot" of tea. While sipping the hot brew, we waited for the next flight line shuttle bus to arrive. I was glad to be back with my squadron mates. It also felt good to be back in a cooler climate.

The air base was full of history. Like the captain had said weeks ago, the RAF used it during World War II. Our aircraft were in fact parked in the exact same spots used by pilots and aircrews back then. I could feel the history, especially while sitting in one of the old flight line shacks during our meetings. Gazing around the room, one could feel as if it were 1941 and we were at war with the Germans. I felt this way often as we flew all around England and touched down at old RAF fields. Most of them looked the same as thirty years before. The old brick and stone buildings seemed to actually exude a profound history.

****

During one morning's briefing, the line chief cautioned us to use proper procedures when conducting engine run tests and to be sure to keep the tower informed by radio as to what we were doing and for how long. Apparently, about a year earlier, a distraught and homesick crew chief determined he had had enough of England. The young sergeant decided to fly his C-130 back home by himself. He was able to start the engines, taxi and take off without being stopped. He flew alone for some time before the order was given to shoot him down. The top brass were afraid he was defecting to the Soviet Union or that he would crash trying to land somewhere.

We made sure we did everything by the book, or should I say checklist. This was much different than the relaxed atmosphere in Turkey.

I quickly got back into the flying rotation and made a few hops to other countries. It was not unusual to have breakfast in England, lunch in Spain and dinner in Italy, all in one day. Each country has its own currency of course, so as we traveled to different areas, I began collecting English pounds, Italian lire and Spanish pesetas. Eventually, I would be trying to pay for a meal in England with lire, or buying a souvenir in Greece with kroner from Denmark. I used different pockets of my flight suit for different countries. Let's see, we're in Greece now, so use lower right leg pocket for drachma. Despite my efforts, it was very confusing.

****

We flew into Aviano air base in Northern Italy one time, landing very late at night. After buttoning down the plane and a taxi ride to the hotel, we fell fast asleep. We were all awakened hours later by one of the guys. He was shouting, "Oh, look at that will ya! Come on, check this out!" Unseen the previous night because of darkness, but plainly visible from our hotel balcony, were the Swiss Alps! They were very majestic. That new morning, we ate breakfast outside on the veranda. We watched some old ladies line up across the street, most with containers on their heads. I asked our waitress what they were doing. She said they got their day's supply of milk each morning and would line up early every morning this way. Milk was in short supply, and not all of the women would come away with their containers full. It was a small reminder of how fortunate we are in the United States. We take so much for granted without realizing.

On that particular trip, we wandered the narrow cobblestone streets and looked in the shop windows. I saw for the first time, the famous globe bars that were so popular. I knew I would have to get one sooner or later.

Back in England one night, while sipping a few beers at the local pub, an attractive brunette approached our table and invited us to a party. She pointed to her girlfriends across the room and they smiled and waved in return. The brunette gave us directions and told us what time to be there. Later our group piled into a couple of taxis and, driving down the left side of the road, traveled a few miles to where we thought we should be. John Forsberg and I were about to be lost! It was dark and foggy. We had gotten out of the cab, and realized as it drove way, we must be in the wrong spot!

We backtracked a little and saw that the road we wanted was across a large field. The field had a sturdy fence all around it, as far as we could see. Thick fog was rolling in. John joked about being chased by a bull or something if we went across. We were late for the party and decided what the hell. Listening one last time in the mist for heavy breathing, John and I looked at each other and gently slid between the boards of the fence.

Once on the other side we slowly began walking, still not sure what was in front of us. We decided it was much wiser to move rapidly, so we started to run in the dark fog. About two-thirds of the way across, John said he heard a tinkling bell and heavy breathing. He held his arm out in front of me to stop us. At first all I heard was our own heavy breathing. Then with a jolt, I heard a bell and heavy snorts coming from our right. In a split second we felt the ground tremble as we heard the charge of pounding hoofs! We both looked at each other in the darkness and took off running full speed. I dared not look back as it might slow me down. I ran faster than I thought I could, even though the ground was very uneven.

Both of us could feel the pounding hoofs gaining on us. "It" was about ten yards behind us and closing, when we finally came into view of the fence. Now we could even hear the heavy breathing as the animal got closer.

Diving through the fence, I rolled on the ground. We just made it through the boards and the safety of the other side. As I turned around on my knees, I saw before me a large black bull! He was snorting and digging at the ground. It was obvious he wanted a piece of us for invading his territory. Wow! That was too close. John looked over at me as we lay panting in the darkness and burst out laughing.

We finally found the house and were relived to discover the party was still ongoing. The guys outnumbered the girls two to one, but we had a good time. I was surprised though by the way they heated the entire house. This became a topic because as the night wore on, we were getting colder. Of course someone suggested turning up the heat. There it was turn "on" the heat. I noticed a small heater in the living room that had a receptacle for coins. Instead of paying a monthly bill, these folks would simply put coins in the slot to keep it running. Unfortunately, no one had any English coins, and it got colder. I had a few coins from other countries, but the girls didn't want to risk breaking the heater. A group of us spent the night huddled together to keep warm. Some party!

A couple of days later, my airplane was on the schedule for a flight to Copenhagen. This trip was looked upon as an R&R event. We brought along a number of non-flying personnel from our squadron, so they could get away from England for a while. The first thing we noticed upon landing in Denmark was the Danish Army troops. They all had long hair! Most of us young troops envied them for that. We stayed two days in Copenhagen and visited the porno shops, the museums and the famous Little Mermaid. Our bedding in the hotel was very soft and fluffy—it felt like sleeping on clouds. The whole trip was relaxing and fun. Before long, however, it was back to England.

****

I tried one day to call Denise back in the States, using one of the famous red phone booths, but never got through to her. The phone kept taking my money but wasn't making the connection. After awhile, I gave up in disgust.

Our quarters in the new barracks had four to a room, and the other three guys in my room were smoking grass almost every night. I had tried marijuana a couple of times before joining the Air Force and found the effects enjoyable. However, now it was completely different. The military put strict rules on the use of marijuana and had very severe penalties if caught. I did not want to risk it, so I chose not to participate. I do remember reclining in bed while the other three listened to music and smoked away. The room was usually a cloud of smoke. I'm surprised no one was ever caught.

Our two-month TDY was up and it was time to pack our bags and head back to the United States. Again, two C-130s flew out one day ahead of the rest of us to get set up in Goose Bay, Labrador.

We flew out with the first main group and made the long journey west across the Atlantic. Snow was on the ground at Goose Bay, but we only stayed overnight and continued on down to Texas the next morning. We were the first aircraft to arrive back at Dyess and were met by our wives and families.

My first rotation had certainly been an adventure, but it was good to be home again.

FIVE

Stateside

I T WAS NOT LONG BEFORE WE GOT BACK TO FLYING around the United States for a variety of missions. In fact, for long stretches, I was away from home more often than not. I was doing a lot of fixing and flying. Denise wasn't too happy about my being away, but she understood. Besides, we had established friends here and had their support. John Rhett had introduced us to his lovely wife, Lynn. She and Denise hit it off right away. When possible we got together for picnics or small parties. John Forsberg was always a fixture. Sometimes he was the only single in a sea of married couples. He loved the attention and typically was a real ham.

I was given my own C-130, number 63-7805. This was the same aircraft that carried the "red cross" mission into Amman. I knew it inside and out. I was no longer an assistant crew chief, but now a crew chief in my own right.

I was promoted to sergeant and now had two young Airmen working for me as my assistants. I stenciled my name above the crew entrance door of my C-130. This was the custom among crew chiefs established long before I arrived. I was only too happy to finally paint my name on my own Hercules. "Sergeant Combs, Crew Chief " it read. White letters painted over a black square. Yes, I was proud.

****

We made a short trip once to Fort Campbell, Kentucky, home of the famous 101st Airborne "Screaming Eagles." We were here to provide some Army troops with their first actual parachute jump. On the first day, while marshaling my aircraft to a spot for the airborne troops, I was caught in the C-130's prop wash. The hot air blew over me with a rush. It blew my hat off and over to the feet of the Army platoon.

The jump school students were standing at attention in Basic Training mode while waiting to board the airplane. Not wanting to disturb them, I walked casually over to their formation and leaned down to pick up my hat. It lay neatly between the first and second row of troops. As I was leaning over however, my sunglasses fell off and crashed to the pavement. Some large sparkling pieces now covering the spit shined boot of the nearest troop. Being as cool as I could be, I reached down for my hat and my now broken sunglasses. I stuffed my hat in my back pocket and put my shades back on my face, one lens on and the other still on the ground in pieces. I walked in front of the whole platoon to where some of my fellow crew chiefs were sitting in a nearby jeep. My friends were howling with laughter. I didn't hear a peep out of any of the Army guys, but I could imagine they were all getting a good chuckle at this Air Force weenie!

The Army guys were a crazy bunch. Once airborne, as we were coming up to their drop zone they began whooping and hollering and pounding on each other. One guy had a pair of ladies panties on his head sticking out from under his helmet. I watched them stand up, hook up to the static line and file out the paratroop doors one at a time shouting "Geronimo!" or "Airborne!"

The area we were flying over was rich in Civil War history. Our copilot was pointing out various battlefields as we flew over them. He really knew his history and explained in detail the battles that had raged below us. During the drops I wanted to be where the action was, so I usually left the flight deck to join the loadmaster, as he readied the paratroop platforms. I was glad to be here with my aircraft and not one of these Army troops preparing to jump. By the looks on their faces though, I think some of them would prefer to stay as well. On each trip to the drop zone I scanned their faces searching for my cousin, Gerry. I had no idea where he was now, but I expected him to suddenly reach out and grab me once we were airborne. Some of the troops had their faces painted making their identities difficult, so if he was on my plane I would hope he'd see me first. We made numerous drops over a period of a few hours that first day.

On the second day, while airborne and about ten minutes from the drop zone, my assistant came up to the flight deck pulling a can of vegetable soup out from under his fatigue jacket. He opened it and placed it into the small galley oven. Before I could say anything, he said, "Watch this." He took a big mouthful of warm soup and backed down the flight deck stairs. As he moved among the Army troops, he suddenly grabbed a plastic bag from his pocket and spit out the soup as if he were throwing up. This caused a chain reaction among the paratroops and soon a dozen or more were heaving into barf bags! His little joke backfired on him. I had him hosing down the cargo floor once we were back on the ground.

It was at this time at Fort Campbell, that Lieutenant Calley was on trial for his actions in Vietnam for the Me Lai massacre. The base was a madhouse of reporters and photographers. The on-base housing was full. We stayed at a little motel just off the base and one of the luxuries of that motel was the vibrating bed. For a quarter, you could lie back and blissfully fall asleep to the soft vibrations. One of the guys staying with us decided he could prolong the effect by kicking the little box that controlled the vibrator. He did all right. The bed would not stop shaking. It bounced and hummed all night long. When we woke up the next morning, he was sleeping on the floor, next to the still moving mattress.

****

Back at Dyess I had a major change in my life. My daughter, Tracy, was born in the base hospital and made me the proudest father ever. We had a crib set up for her in our little two-bedroom house. Mom flew down from Seattle for a few days to help us.

One morning during Mom's visit, we woke up to discover little black bugs invading us from the area around a big tree in the back yard. I had never seen so many insects at one time and they wanted in! I sprayed insecticide all around the back door and the patio beyond. Still the bugs marched on. We discovered a few inside the house and redoubled our efforts. I sprayed all around the tree and all over the thousands of tiny bugs who by now had climbed the back wall of the house. Nothing seemed to work. Suddenly one morning they just disappeared. I have no idea what they were and they never bothered us again. Still, we battled an occasional cockroach now and again, but we were used to that by now.

I just couldn't get used to the humidifier, though. Our little house didn't have regular air conditioning, just this one old machine hanging in the bedroom window. Each night, Denise and I would quickly pull back the covers of the bed to catch any lingering cockroaches. The sheets were always damp from the humidifier. Take your clean sheets out of the washer and put them on your bed without drying them first and you'll get the idea.

Shortly after Mom left, we got the bill in the mail from the hospital. Tracy's delivery cost $8.00! I just couldn't stop looking at her precious tiny features. I looked forward to leaving the flight line and coming home to my family. Tracy was just too cute!

Our flying schedule picked up and I had to leave for a few days. My aircraft, along with John Forsberg's (who was also now a crew chief), made the flight east. John's aircraft serial number was 63-816 and mine was 63-805. Normally we parked next to each other on the Dyess flight line. On this trip we eventually ended up at Eglin AFB in Florida. I remembered it well. This was the place I had gotten into trouble for not saluting the general.

It was late when we touched down, and well past midnight by the time I had finished my post-flight inspection. John and I, along with our assistants, went to base operations to find a place to sleep for the night. We discovered that nothing was available either on or off the base. As we roamed the terminal, deciding what to do, John tried the door to the VIP lounge and found it unlocked. We looked around and quickly hustled inside, closing the door behind us. What a place! The room was stocked with fresh fruit and baskets of breads and crackers. There were sodas and beer in a cooler. We dove in and enjoyed a real feast. We ended up sleeping on the red leather couches and woke up early to avoid being detected. As we sauntered out to the flight line and our waiting aircraft, we left behind a lounge devoid of any food or drink. We laughed when we thought about some colonel walking his guests into that room expecting to find it well stocked as we had. We left a few dollars on the table to cover our meal.

We flew out that morning and headed to Forbes AFB in Kansas. Snow flurries greeted us as we touched down on the runway. By the time the "follow me" truck had us parked, it was snowing heavily. We checked with base operations and soon realized we were going to be stuck here. A few of us built a snowman outside base operations, while the rest of the crew found a place for us to stay.

We were assigned comfortable rooms. They were large rooms, each with four beds and a desk. After a meal at the chow hall, we went back and tried to get some sleep. I kept squirming all night long. My feet were cold and I tucked in the covers and pulled my legs up to the fetal position. I was still cold at my feet. At first light, I discovered why. A window had been left open and it snowed all night. The result was a few inches of snow on the foot of my bed! Looking out the open window, we could not even see the building next door. It was a blizzard. Someone knocked on our door. It was the copilot of John Forsberg's plane. He said because of the blizzard outside, most of the base is being shut down. We had permission to go to the Officer's Club, which was across the street, and hang out there. At least we could get a hot meal. As we trekked the short distance to the Officer's Club, I walked straight into a tree! I could not see a thing in all the blowing snow.

Inside the club it was nice and warm and full of officers and pilots. They treated us very kindly and made sure we were fed. We didn't have to pay for the food either. It was great! I played pool with a one-star general and we all watched "The Blue Max," a story about a World War I fighter pilot. I couldn't think of a more appropriate group to watch that movie with. My pool partner, the general, was a World War II fighter pilot.

Captives of the still raging snowstorm, we passed the time telling war stories. This experience was absolutely amazing. Some of the older pilots told stories that gave me goose bumps. Some stories were about heroism, valor, death and destruction, while others were humorous. By the second day sequestered there in the club it became my "turn" for a story. So, with a Kansas blizzard blowing outside, the pilots and flight crews began to circle around me with their chairs, jockeying for position. Fresh beers were passed around. Of course, I felt I had little to offer, compared with the stories we had all shared these past hours.

I told them the story of our hostage snatch in Jordan. Surprisingly, they all liked the tale and said it was worthy. The general stood up and said in a deep tone, "We place ourselves in harm's way not for ourselves, but for others because our country makes the request. To do so is admirable. It doesn't matter that shells were fired or not, it's combat just the same. Some of my scariest missions were like that." Someone in our group ordered another round of beers as the general spoke. "That reminds me," he continued, "did I ever tell you guys about the time I flew a U-2 over the fence out of Incirlik? I think it was spring of 1961..."

After two days of playing officer again, we were finally able to scrape the snow off our aircraft and get back into the air. We launched and headed west, landing at Nellis AFB in Nevada. Once I had completed the work on my airplane, I went to base operations and called the International Hotel in downtown Las Vegas. "Yes," I was told, "Elvis is performing two shows tonight. Would you prefer tickets to the dinner or cocktail show?" The dinner show we discovered was too expensive. Two of us decided just then to head downtown. We would grab a room at a Motel Six and see Elvis' cocktail show after a quick meal somewhere.

We checked into our motel, showered and put on civilian clothes. After a burger, we caught a cab to the International and got in line for the show. Once inside, the waitress asked us what we wanted to drink. She returned a short time later and proceeded to fill up our table with glasses. I was not quite sure what was happening. Included in the admission price were three drinks each. The waitress would not serve during the show, so we got them all before the event started.

What a show it was! We had great seats. I felt as if I could almost reach out and touch Elvis, we were that close. He sounded great, too, mixing old songs with new.

Women screamed as he moved all over the stage. I had a great time! I'm sure it was a two-hour show but it went by quickly and seemed to end much too soon. We roamed around Vegas awhile, taking in the sights before heading back to our motel. I realized how good it felt to step back into to the civilian world, even if only for a night.

Early the next morning we conducted our preflight inspection and flew on to California, stopping at George AFB and Edwards AFB. From there, we made our way back to Texas.

****

Flying in my own aircraft became a great joy. Sometimes we would land at a civilian airport and draw quite a crowd as we taxied past the terminal in our camouflaged C-130. Many folks would stop us in the terminal asking questions about this or that. Most just wanted to know what kind of airplane we flew.

I was confident in my ability to maintain my aircraft and had performed a number of tasks to keep mine in the air. By now, I knew every inch of that C-130 inside and out, nose to tail. I had changed the brakes and tires, replaced pumps and valves, been inside the wing dry bays and on top of the fuselage. I documented every action and signed it off. I was quick to remedy the write-ups made by the pilot or flight engineer.

Abilene had become a home away from home. Denise was doing well as an Air Force wife and as a mother to Tracy. When I was not on interstate trips, we had a home life filled with friends and activities. We took Tracy proudly to church on Sundays and had her baptized. Denise and I would often attend the dances or play bingo at the community center at Dyess.

****

One morning, I emerged through the top hatch of my aircraft to see a giant C-5 transport on final approach. I watched as the new jumbo cargo plane drew closer to the ground. With a screeching of about twenty tires the jet landed, reversing its huge engines to slow down. Later that morning, I roamed over to the C-5 now parked on the flight line. I struck up a conversation with the technical sergeant who was her crew chief. He gladly gave me a tour of his impressive aircraft. After we explored the enormous cargo deck we went upstairs. Here we would find the passenger area and the large flight deck. This airplane was amazing inside and out! After saying goodbye to her chief, I went back to my C-130. Comparatively, my aircraft was much smaller and now felt almost confined, but I wouldn't change places with the C-5's crew chief.

During this period of time, John Forsberg had joined up with some others in our squadron's parachute club. He had gone through the training and made a handful of actual jumps. With each jump he became more and more cocky and tried to convince me to join up. Denise was against the idea and basically I could live without it. By now I had watched hundreds of Army troops spill out through my paratroop doors. I was not eager to join them. We carried parachutes in our C-130s and had been taught how to use them. I just figured it would have to be a real emergency for me to think about jumping out of my airplane.

John finally quit hounding me and quit the club, when his main chute failed to open one afternoon. Falling through the sky, John deployed his reserve chute but badly wrenched his back when it snapped open. He was through jumping, and I didn't need any more excuses.

****

One day my aircraft was assigned a flight to Hickam AFB in Hawaii. I enjoyed working with a young Hawaiian Airman who was one of my assistants, and he boasted of the great time he would show us in Hawaii. I was pumped up. On the morning of the flight, Denise and Tracy brought me to the Dyess flight line and we said our goodbyes. I started to preflight the aircraft. I refueled and made sure our oxygen supply was full. I checked all the systems of my airplane. Once it was completed, the aircrew began to arrive. I was ready to go, but I didn't.

Every squadron has one pain in the ass, maybe even more than one.

Ours was Staff Sergeant Dillrod. No one liked him. He was what we called, a "lifer." He had tried to make it on the outside but could not. So he re-enlisted, only he was rarely promoted. He had been in the Air Force forever, but was only one rank above me. That's all he needed.

Dillrod decided at the last moment that he wanted to take this trip. . . and be in charge! Now it was my aircraft and I was still its crew chief and would have authority, but Dillrod could and would make it difficult. What was an exciting and anticipated trip was now a pain in the ass. After discussions with the line chief, I relinquished my aircraft to SSgt. Dillrod for this short trip, provided Dillrod repaired all discrepancies that I found on post-flight, once they returned. Dillrod agreed, but he shouldn't have. Reluctantly, I called Denise to drive back to base and pick me up…I would not be going to Hawaii. Days later when they came back, I met them at the aircraft and started my post-flight inspection. There are some tasks on board a C-130 that are less desirable than others, like inspection and cleaning of urinals. I had Dillrod busy for a week doing all the menial dirty tasks that my assistants had been putting off doing. The line chief backed me up all the way.

****

Tornadoes are relatively common in parts of Texas, so it was not unusual to receive warning about pending storms. One such storm caught us by surprise, and before we knew it, we had driving rain and very high winds. This required us to go out to our aircraft and chain them down to the ground. I drove the Ford Econoline truck (just like the one in Turkey) between the rows of C-130s as the wind and rain whipped up around me. We had sixteen airplanes in our squadron, and it quickly became a race against time and the elements.

Moving down the second row of C-130s, I came to John Forsberg's plane, number 816. He jumped down from the flight deck as I approached. We chained his down first and then he jumped into the truck to help me with the rest of the aircraft. As we approached one C-130 with the winds behind us, I opened the door…only to have the wind catch it! I watched as it swung 270 degrees around smashing against the windshield, which cracked. Before it could swing back, the door dropped to the ground. John and I looked at each other and burst out laughing. I grabbed the door and threw it into the bed of the truck. We continued to drive around the flight line minus the driver's door. I got drenched just driving the truck.

Finally, we finished chaining down the remaining C-130s. I radioed back to operations to let them know the task was complete and with a pause added, "Oh, the door fell off." The line chief was beside himself with anger once he saw the damage. "How could you treat government property this way?" he demanded. I tried to explain that it was an accident.

Sergeant Forsberg got into the conversation and said he saw it happen. John tried to tell the chief that it happened as I explained. The chief got madder still and said John and I would lose a stripe over this. John surprised me and got in the chief 's face and said, "You want this stripe? Here, take it!" With that, John using his right hand, reached across to his left shoulder and ripped off his sergeant's and threw it to the line chief. I was stunned. The line chief looked directly at John, now half-a-sergeant. Instead of more anger, he began to try to calm John down. "Now Sergeant Forsberg," he said "don't get upset, we'll handle this."

That was the end of it. John was incensed that we would be held responsible and he was not going to stand for it. He risked more than his stripe to make his point. He was a good friend.

****

I had attracted some attention around Abilene with my custom painted Corvette. Most had never seen anything like it (I don't think there was anything like it!). Anyway, a local merchant asked me one day if I would like to show it. Abilene was hosting their first custom car show in the new Taylor County Coliseum and I was invited.

Denise and I spent a few days cleaning and polishing to make it ready. John Forsberg helped with our display. In fact we used a large carpet from his living room to place under the car! It was his idea. The car show was fun and I picked up two trophies, "Best in Class" and "Most Unusual

Paint." The famous drag racer Shirley Cha-Cha Muldowney was a feature at the show, along with her race car. She wandered by one evening and after looking my Corvette over, said she thought the paint job looked like an aerial view of a golf course. I took it as a compliment. The scheme was the idea of an old family friend, Bob Walters. We had painted the car with five coats of a light green. Then, using four different shades of green, we applied single coats of each shade, twice! By gently sanding through the thin layers we exposed patterns in different shapes and colors. It was unusual. In all, the scheme was five different shades of green in a very high gloss mosaic. Sort of like colored wood-grain.

Soon after the diversion of the car show, I was scheduled for a trip up to Alaska. I thought this would be fun because we would fly over my home state of Washington. Hours into the flight, we crossed the state on our way north. It was bittersweet to see home but not be home. With all four C-130s flying in trail over Washington, the navigator radioed back to Sgt. Forsberg's plane. I pointed out landmarks to John and his crew as well as my own crew. The Cascade Mountains were spectacular! I was proud to call the land beneath us my true home.

We touched down at Elmendorf AFB outside Anchorage during a snowstorm. John's plane almost flew into a mountain and the whole crew was visibly shaken. They were on approach in zero visibility when a mountaintop rushed into view! Both pilot and copilot pulled back on the stick and the aircraft lurched up and over at the last second! John was quite excited and we tried to calm him down. After a while, he was his old self again. "Hell John," I teased, "you could have put on your parachute and simply jumped!" He smiled and reached for his back, as he let out a fake groan of pain. He was still hurting from his last parachute sport jump.

By the time we had finished performing the maintenance on our aircraft, everything on base had shut down. No midnight snack bar was available and for us, no place to sleep. We could not get into Anchorage because of the storm. Eight of us trudged back to our four waiting C-130s, four crew chiefs and four assistants.

We passed two LC-130s on our way out. These are the ski-equipped versions of the C-130, with large skis attached to the main landing gear and a smaller pair mounted to the nose gear. We talked shop awhile with their crew chiefs, comparing our aircraft. Shortly after, it was back to our airplanes. We would sleep in our aircraft, although none of us got much in the way of real sleep. Once inside my airplane, we grabbed the curtains from around the commode in the cargo bay. This is what we would use for blankets. We lay on the bunks in the flight deck and huddled. When it got too cold, one of us would jump down from his bunk and approach the engineer's overhead panel. There he would start the sequence of twisting dials to fire up the gas turbine engine or GTC. This would provide bleed air and heat to the flight deck. When it got real toasty, we would shut down the GTC and try to fall back to sleep. It seemed however that at any given time, at least one of the four C-130s had its GTC running and that kept us all awake. It stopped snowing long enough for us to leave the next day, and I slept in my bunk most of the way back.

Off the west coast somewhere, we encountered two C-130s from Dyess on their way up to Alaska. We passed nose to nose, with our aircraft at a higher altitude. I hoped those guys would have better luck finding a place to stay.

Back at Dyess we learned that the two C-130 squadrons had earned Outstanding Unit Citation awards for our rescue mission in Amman, Jordan. Around our squadron, we were treated as celebrities. It seemed for a short while anyway.

****

One afternoon during a severe hailstorm, I incurred the wrath of some officer by parking my Corvette in an empty C-130 hanger. I tried to explain that I only sought temporary shelter to protect the custom paint from certain damage. It was against regulations, and he kept insisting that I move it. I argued with the officer just long enough to avoid trouble, and the worst of the raging storm outside. I was angry with this snob. So, once the giant hanger doors were opened, I demonstrated to the captain what 300 horsepower converted to the ground looks like! I never saw the guy again. No sense of humor.

****

It was my turn to tow my aircraft over to the wash rack one day and give it a thorough bath. Washing a C-130 is neither quick nor easy. The dark streaks from my four jet engines were the most difficult to clean. We were constantly working overhead, as in under the wings looking up, or under the fuselage on a roller. It seemed no matter how much protective gear we wore, some of the solvent based cleaner would get on our hands or arms. Later that night, home and in bed, I tossed and turned. My forearms were in flames. They were both crimson red and it was obvious that the solvents had burned them.

Early the next morning, I checked into the dispensary. The nurses had me soak my arms in a warm soapy solution for some time. They bandaged up both arms and wrists including my hands. I really mean bandaged too! I felt like a mummy. I had driven myself here, but now there was no possible way I could drive home. I had to call a couple of my friends living on base, to come get me and get my car home. I convalesced for a week or so then was ready to get back to flying.

My aircraft and a few others were targeted for a return trip to Pope AFB in North Carolina. I can say for sure that mine was the cleanest C-130 there. It was not however, the meanest. We parked near three MC-130 Combat Talon aircraft. They had the Fulton recovery system scissors on the nose and were painted black and very dark green. These were Special Operations aircraft filled with plenty of electronics.

They were guarded closely by the Air Police. I wondered what it was like to be the crew chief on one of them. Pretty hot stuff!

****

On one of our local flights around Dyess one day, the copilot got up from his seat and told me to sit down. I had by now, the ability to perform the C-130 engine start and taxi procedures. I had, of course, run my own engines numerous times and lately had taxied to the edge of the runway for tests on some occasions. I had not, however, been given the opportunity to actually *fly* one. I wish I could say it was exhilarating, but since we were flying straight and narrow, I couldn't deviate much from that at the time. It was a thrill however, knowing for a brief period I had control over all that power. The C-130 is known as the Hercules for good reason. Still, this was my airplane and I was flying it. I felt like I had come a long way. Often, at times like those, I wished Dad were alive.

We practiced landings for weeks on the dirt strip next to Dyess' main runway. Some of the landings we made were more like a touch and go! I made the mistake once, of standing up during a copilots' landing. The aircraft bounced and tilted as we performed a kind of controlled crash. I was tossed around the back of the flight deck. I barely made it to the lower bunk and the safety of my seatbelt. Another lesson learned.

Another time, we performed a JATO takeoff using the special "clip-on" Jet Assist Takeoff bottles. It's sort of like having a supercharger attached to your car. We climbed at a very steep angle and were in the clouds in no time. It may sound dramatic, but it felt like being in a rocket ship. Wow!

I was not always required to fly with my airplane when it was on these local training missions. So one day while our planes were in the air, Sgt. Forsberg and I wandered over to the nearest B-52 and went inside. For such a huge airplane, it was very cramped. This machine was all business, however, and we were glad no one saw us go in or come out. It was on the wash rack and the guards were gone.

****

We performed maintenance on our aircraft and kept them flying. We did brake repairs and wheel changes. We changed engines and tore up the entire floor to get access to flight controls for adjustments and upgrades. My aircraft had been painted months before back in England, after our "red cross" mission, so I no longer was sporting the huge white squares with red crosses.

One evening just before dusk, I discovered during my preflight that I had a light out in the tail. We were scheduled to lift off in less than one hour, so I called squadron operations for a crane or cherry picker. Fifteen minutes later, it was parked at the rear of my plane. Walking outside, under the wings of my C-130, I suddenly noticed the weather was turning ominous. I had only minutes to replace the light in the navigational beacon on top of the vertical stabilizer. Apprehensively, I entered the little white box and closed the "door" behind me. With the help of another crew chief, I was hoisted up in the cherry picker. There I was, about three stories up in that tiny box and the wind and rain starts. My platform was bouncing in the wind and I was trying not to drop the small screw in my slippery hand. If I got too close with the picker, I'd have damaged the tail. I had to reach "waaay out." I got the light changed and made it back down again, but it was a wild ride! I signaled to the driver of the line truck that I was finished with the crane. He acknowledged my signal and reached for his microphone. At this point the wind was howling and the rain fell almost horizontally. I was soaking wet. As I was retreating into my aircraft, the line truck pulled up again. I knew he wasn't going to leave his comfy seat, so I ran back into the rain and wind to see what he wanted. The severe weather had required operations to cancel the flight, he explained. We went about making sure all the aircraft were properly chained down.

****

One afternoon I had the task of hoisting my aircraft with hydraulic jacks. I attached the two front jack points with bolts to the forward fuselage just below the pilot and copilot windows. A small (relatively) jack is used on each side. Two larger jacks are attached under the wings, one on each side and between the engines. In a carefully planned operation the aircraft is raised. In this position we could perform landing gear checks and maintenance. It was strange to see my aircraft poised as if in flight, just a few feet off the ground. It looked like a giant model on a stand.

I took great pride in my airplane and kept it in almost perfect shape. I did not have any aborts due to maintenance, and for that I was proud. It was enjoyable sitting up in the flight deck while working on the aircraft forms. The hum of electricity and various avionics units created a soothing atmosphere. I could look out the flight deck window and see the other crew chiefs moving about their charges or alone in their flight decks attending to paperwork as well.

If a potential life threatening condition existed on the aircraft, I would mark its status in the aircraft maintenance book. If I were grounding the aircraft, it would be under a red X. If it had a persistent problem like a sticky valve or something that was not life threatening, it carried a red diagonal. As the crew chief, I had the authority to keep the airplane on the ground if I thought its problem severe enough. I took pride in minimizing my own down time and kept mine flying. When problems did come up, I quickly took care of them.

SIX

Second Rotation

W E WERE APPROACHING THE SUMMER OF 1971 and time for the
squadron to go on TDY rotation to Germany. Again we would fly
missions throughout Europe in support of NATO. Denise and Tracy
brought me to the flight line, and we said our goodbyes. I conducted a
preflight inspection of my aircraft and made ready. This time I was one
of two C-130s that would precede the whole squadron and be set up in
Goose Bay, Labrador.

We were given accommodations again in the barracks next to the
WAFs and the shows continued. The WAFs knew the guys were
watching and made the most of it. We serviced our squadron's aircraft
as they came and went on their way to Frankfurt, Germany. After a few
days here, we were quite bored. The base had a library and chow hall but
little else. On a dare one night, a couple of us ran across and into the
WAFs barracks and up the stairs. We ran down the halls knocking on
doors and shouting. It seemed risky at the time.

Finally everyone had passed through and we could crank engines and
head for Germany ourselves. We would be based at Rhein Main Air Base
in Frankfurt. Rhein Main was known as "The Gateway to Europe" and
was located near the Black Forest. Being part German myself, I was
looking forward to seeing the land.

Hours later as we approached Frankfurt, I began to notice the castles below us. Old, weathered and full of history, they were an amazing sight from up there. "This is where the Great Hindenburg was kept before the war," said the copilot over interphone. Like the dirigible itself, the huge hanger was long gone. As we circled over Rhein Main, the copilot pointed out the area where the giant blimp had been moored.

Mine was the last of the C-130s to arrive in Germany. We were met at the airplane by squadron mates who would post-flight and refuel for me, so our crew could become settled. We stayed in huge three-story white barracks with cavernous basements. The Germans hid in these basements from Allied bombs during World War II. Some buildings on base still bore the scars of that conflict. Large divots from bomb shrapnel had shaped a number of scars in the sides of many of the old buildings. Large chunks had been taken out of the concrete then painted over. Clearly they could have been filled, but I figured they left them as a sort of badge of honor.

****

As a sergeant, I could now enjoy the NCO clubs at the various bases we would come across, as we flew throughout Europe. The NCO club at Rhein Main was richly appointed and they had stage shows almost every night. We ate dinner there as often as we could.

Within a day or two of our arrival, we were back in the air again, delivering cargo to various bases around Germany. We visited Ramstein, Spangdahlem, Stuttgart and Wueschheim, to name a few. The German countryside was beautiful.

I bought an inexpensive cuckoo clock in Weisbaden to surprise Denise. (We were both surprised when we put it together weeks later in Texas. I was proud to have it out of the box and hanging on the wall. However, we soon discovered our cuckoo bird was only willing to softly say, "coo.") It *was* cute!

****

Forsberg's plane flew a re-supply mission to Berlin and strayed slightly off course and out of the strict flight corridor. He said later that it scared everyone when the Russian MIGs flew in to intercept. John said things were a bit tense for a while, but they got in and back out again without a major incident. His pilot stayed cool through it all. I admired these C-130 pilots. The aircrews I flew with were professionals in every way. It was a mutual trust. We relied on each other.

****

We once flew a mission to Torrejon Air Base outside Madrid. Two other C-130s from our sister squadron were already parked on the flight line. We stayed out late that night checking out the bars. As we left one bar, the three of us were suddenly confronted by a mean looking group of men. There were about ten of them and they were big. I feared the worse. They gathered around us asking if we were American. It seemed we had stumbled onto a champion rugby team in celebration. They were pleased to meet Americans and insisted on buying us drinks. We went back to the bar that we had just left and shared a few with the team. I don't remember what country they were from, but it seems to me it was Eastern Europe somewhere. It turned out to be a great night.

****

I had just encountered a deep sleep back at the transient barracks, when we had to get up and preflight our aircraft. Soon we were airborne and heading east. We landed at Helleniken Air Base just outside of Athens, Greece, with fuel flow restrictor problems in my No. 4 engine. I checked out the problem and soon discovered we would need a new valve to make it operate again. This was not a C-130 base, so no one had the part we needed. We radioed back to our squadron in Germany. I requested a replacement part. They would bring us one, but it would be two days away. We could have flown out on three engines, but we all agreed the sights there were world class. We swam in the Mediterranean and gazed upon the ruins above Athens. They were lit up at night and that made them all the more majestic.

We visited sights around Athens until another C-130 from our squadron arrived with our part and our mail. I became friends with the crew chief. His name was Ike. He was a staff sergeant and a very likable guy; however, he had an embarrassing habit. Ike just couldn't resist straightening pictures on the wall...any wall...any place. Ike would suddenly get up from our table at a fine restaurant and casually walk across the room. He'd excuse himself to the people eating their meal, while he crawled over them to rearrange the picture on the wall. It just drove him nuts to see anything out of alignment.

Back on the flight line, I replaced the valve on No. 4 and put the engine components back together. We performed engine tests to be sure all was well, and we flew out the next morning.

We approached a small landing strip, somewhere in the boot heel of southern Italy. As I stood behind the pilot's seat looking out the flight deck windows, it was apparent this would be a hit-or-miss situation. The runway below us was surrounded on three sides by water and was not made for large aircraft. A C-130 is designed to takeoff and land on short runways, but this left no margin for error. We flew low over the runway to gauge our approach, then circled once and headed in for a landing. We almost sucked water into the intakes with our reverse prop thrust! That had been close, but we made it.

We spent the night in a quaint harbor village. One of the officers treated the crew to dinner that evening We allowed him to sort of pick and choose our entries for us. He said he had been there before and knew what was good. We found out later, our main entree was dog meat! To me, it tasted like venison.

The next morning while preflighting my airplane, we were attacked by a giant swarm of locusts. There were thousands of them. We worried that they would be sucked into the engine intakes and cause damage to all four engines. We delayed our takeoff for a while hoping they would leave. Most of them did. We cranked up two engines to move to the taxiway, pulverizing any remaining locusts with our props as we lumbered over to the runway. This was the time for a JATO assist takeoff, but we didn't have any JATO bottles on board. We backed up to the edge of the runway. The C-130, by the way, is one of very few airplanes that can back up under its own power. I sat on the lower bunk and fastened my seat belt and said a prayer. We set the brakes and brought the four turboprops to maximum power. The aircraft shuddered and strained under the pressure. Finally, the pilot released the brakes and we bounded down the short runway. We lifted off at the last second. Whew! I hoped we wouldn't have to return to that place.

Back in Germany, I found out that I had received orders for Southeast Asia. The orders specified I was to be an IO on board an AC-130 gunship. "What's an IO?" I asked. "An Illuminator Operator," I was told. "You'll operate a searchlight in either standard or infrared mode looking for the bad guys." One of the older and well-seasoned crew chiefs in our squadron had served as an IO the previous year. Later in his room as a few of us sat around, he filled me in completely.

"Picture a football field," he said. "Spectre can lay down a 20mm shell every square foot...with precision...in the dark...with just one orbit and a five second burst from its guns!" I came away wishing I hadn't asked.

My orders were for mid October. Once we completed our TDY in Germany, I would have a short time back at Dyess before heading home on leave, then flying on to Thailand.

Meanwhile, Ike invited me to join him for a little trip off base one afternoon. He had been to Germany before and knew of a small hamlet on the other side of the forest. We walked the half-mile through the trees and bushes to the little town. We enjoyed a few beers and a good meal at a country pub. We were the only Americans in town. Around midnight, we decided to head back to the base. We had not anticipated the total darkness that now surrounded us. No flashlight or lighter in our pockets to illuminate the way. Both of us stumbled back in total darkness, with nothing but memories of the general direction to move. It took us hours to get back, and we were lucky to have made it at all. We were absolutely blind. I walked into numerous trees and tripped over rocks and logs all along the way. We laughed about it later, but it was not at all funny at the time.

****

My C-130 and crew were scheduled to fly an Embassy supply mission to Bucharest, Romania. At this time Romania was still under communist control. We were told we would not be wearing our uniforms. Instead we wore civilian clothes for this unusual trip. We loaded the aircraft with two pallets of supplies and lifted off the next morning. We knew we were over Romanian airspace when we picked up two MIG fighters as escorts. The MIGs were silver in color with red stars on their tails. We complied with their directions.

We landed at the "civilian" airport and off-loaded our cargo. I performed a post-flight inspection of my aircraft and locked it up for the night. The loadmaster and flight engineer stayed behind to assist me. Once finished, the three of us took a taxi to our hotel downtown. There we met with the rest of the crew. We held a briefing and were told not to go anywhere alone, not even the hotel restaurant. Later that evening, we were invited to the American Embassy for a cocktail party. The loadmaster, flight engineer and I took the elevator down to a waiting Embassy staff car. It was dark blue with tinted windows. It so happened that my two companions were both big and very strong. I was squeezed between them in the back seat of the car. On the way to the Embassy, I couldn't help feeling as if I were a VIP surrounded by bodyguards.

The party was stiff and formal. We stood around holding drinks in crystal glasses, while servants offered us dainty foods. We roamed throughout the Embassy garden, mostly among ourselves, talking shop. Thankfully, the party didn't last too long. Back at the hotel we decided to go for a drink on the rooftop bar. We enjoyed a few beers and watched the Romanians dance. I was tired and decided to grab the elevator back down to our room. The others were going to stay awhile, so I ventured on my own. (I know, we weren't supposed to...)

I got on the elevator and it descended, but suddenly stopped. The door opened and two men got inside. We said nothing as the door closed and I waited for the feel of a gun in my side. I decided I didn't want these guys to know which floor I was on, so I rode all the way down to the lobby. We all got out and I spun around and quickly pushed the button to close the door. I rode up alone, thinking I had evaded capture. They were probably just a couple of businessmen on holiday, but I had no way of knowing. My roommates had returned. So we settled in for the night, still being careful of our conversations. We were briefed earlier to expect that our rooms were probably bugged. With all this communist cloak and dagger stuff going on, I didn't sleep well that night.

Early the next morning I went downstairs to the main cafeteria for breakfast. I had checked out the gift shop already, looking for those small souvenir spoons that I had been collecting for Mom. They didn't have any. However, as I finished my breakfast, I noticed the small sugar spoon on the table. I took it to the cashier and tried to explain to her, that I wanted to buy the spoon, as well as pay for my breakfast. No one spoke English, so I had a difficult time conveying my intentions. I paid extra for the spoon and left the cashier, still shaking her head.

We grabbed a couple of taxis and headed back to the airport. The taxi brought us onto to the airport flight line. The driver continued right up to the wing tip of my airplane. He left us along with our bags, in the shade of my right wing. Someone from the Embassy was supposed to meet us at the airplane, but he hadn't arrived yet.

I decided I would go ahead and start my preflight inspection while the rest were waiting. I walked around the back of the aircraft and to the left paratroop door. As I began to unlock the padlock placed there the night before, I noticed a large circle of wax. It was on my left, about halfway up the door-track and out of my reach. The wax was bright red with a special seal stamped on it. If I opened the door, I would obviously break the seal.

I had the padlock in my hand when I heard shouts behind me. I turned to face a Romanian guard standing about thirty feet away. He was shouting something, as he motioned for me to move away from the aircraft, with a sweep of his rifle. He was speaking Romanian or Russian, so I had no idea what he was saying. I glared back at him. My first thought was, "Who is this guy to tell me to move away from *my own* airplane?" He grew more insistent and gestured again with his rifle, for me to move away. I got the point. As I turned back to the paratroop door to put the lock back on, he shouted again, only louder. This time though, he swung around his AK-47 rifle. Very slowly and with intent, he aimed his rifle right at me! Instead of being afraid, I got angry. I started walking toward him still holding the lock in my left hand, as he shouted again. This time he flipped the safety off just above the trigger and placed me squarely in his sights. I remember seeing his finger on the trigger. I continued to walk slowly towards him, keeping my eyes focused on his.

About this time, the Embassy staff car rolled up and the guy who had put the seal on the airplane ran over to check it. He said something to the guard, who slowly lowered his weapon. I stopped, but I continued to glare defiantly at the guard. If the staff car hadn't shown up when it did, I'm not sure what might have happened. I wanted the guard to know it was my airplane, that's all. What was I going to do, throw the lock at him? Walking up to him was, of course, a threat. At what distance would he have fired? I gave him one last hard look then turned around. By this time my aircrew had come around the back of the C-130 and escorted me to the area under the right wing, where our bags lay.

"Sergeant Combs, you almost got yourself killed! What the hell were you doing?" the flight engineer asked.

"I'm just trying to do my job," I told him. The guard had pissed me off.

With the seal formally broken, I was able to get the aircraft opened up and begin my preflight inspection. The guard marched away into obscurity. During the whole flight back to Germany, the aircrew talked about the "International Incident" that almost happened. At least I had my souvenir spoon!

****

Back in Germany, Ike and I took a trip to downtown Frankfurt. We saw Grand Funk Railroad and Humble Pie in concert. The whole event was weird. The announcer between songs would speak German to all the fans, then the group would play and sing, of course, in English. Even after being around jet engines all this time, my ears were ringing for days from the loud music.

My aircraft and crew took another mission to Aviano Air base in northern Italy.

This was the base located close to the Swiss Alps and was very scenic. This time through, I bought a globe bar. The gray-haired merchant used a donkey cart to haul it back to the airplane. I stored it in the forward cargo area. I noticed the old man was as comfortable there on the flight line as he was in his store. It was obvious he had done this many times before. I thanked the old man, offered him a small tip and began my preflight.

We flew on to Iraklion Air Base in Crete. Here we met up with a couple other C-130s from our squadron. While on the ground, I walked over to the one small building near the airstrip and started looking for a souvenir spoon. I had no real expectations way out there but figured I'd look anyway. Surprise! There in this little old dusty building, I found a quaint gift shop with an amazing array of souvenirs. I had no cash, but the merchant let me write a check! This guy was a real entrepreneur. I grabbed my spoon and headed back to my airplane. One of the other C-130s had drained its batteries, and with no ground power units available, he was unable to start his engines. We positioned my aircraft directly in front of the other C-130 and produced enough prop wash to windmill their props and get them going. Somewhat like compression starting your car.

Making our way back towards Germany, we stopped for the night at Torrejon Air Base in Spain. This time I stayed on base and got to bed early. The next morning we cranked engines and taxied out for takeoff, only to shut down again. I was helping the loadmaster in back and inquired over the intercom as to what the problem was. "We'll hold here for an IFE," the pilot responded. An IFE was an in-flight emergency. I climbed the stairs to the flight deck and watched out the windows as an F-4 Phantom jet came in with its landing gear still retracted. Fire crews had to put foam on the runway to soften his landing. We had a front row seat as the Phantom slid sideways down the runway. The canopy came up and the two pilots fell out and ran away from the foam-covered jet. We all held our breath for the fire that never came. We started engines again and took off using an alternate runway.

****

Back in Germany again the squadron prepared for our return trip back to Texas. Our two-month TDY was over and it was time to go home. Two of our aircraft left a day early to become set up in Goose Bay.

While waiting for the return trip, I spent some time at the base theater. The movie was called "That's The Way It Is." It was about Elvis Presley's Las Vegas shows. I watched the movie repeatedly. It was like being there again and seeing the same show all over. It made me homesick. But I kept coming back ("One ticket, please!").

Before long it was our turn to start engines and head for home. I had my globe bar firmly strapped down in the forward cargo area, and we were at maximum takeoff weight with everyone else's souvenirs. One pilot had even acquired a 30-caliber machine gun mounted on a tripod. With our baggage, support equipment and "toys" we took off and headed west towards the Atlantic. I slept in my bunk most of the way.

I woke up to notice the navigator frantically going over his charts and slide rules.

The flight engineer was tapping the fuel gauges on his overhead panel. We had encountered severe head winds and were running out of fuel. As I looked out the flight deck window I saw no land in sight. The copilot asked me if we had our full complement of life rafts in the wings. I began to realize how serious this was. "This will be close," the navigator told us solemnly. The pilot suggested we lighten our load to gain an extra margin. Some of the gear we were carrying belonged to guys who were flying back on other aircraft. They wouldn't know it but we were about to make them very unhappy. I went back to the cargo area and the loadmaster opened the rear door and lowered the ramp to horizontal. The pilot came on the loudspeaker for those riding with us who did not have headphones and explained our situation.

We began pushing equipment off the ramp, watching it tumble as it slowly dropped into the Atlantic Ocean. The young captain who owned the machine gun was beside himself and tried to stop us from throwing his valuable possession overboard. The pilot told him that it was either him or the gun...it was entirely his choice! He stood back helpless as we pushed it over the edge. We continued to jettison our cargo including a couple other globe bars. I was resigned with the knowledge that mine would go out too. Considering the alternative, I was prepared to push it out along with the others. We had purged about a third of our cargo when the pilot informed us we were close to the Arctic Circle and he had Keflavik Naval Air Station, Iceland, in sight. We closed the cargo ramp and door. I went back up to the flight deck and strapped myself in on the lower bunk.

With a lighter load and in descent, the pilot shut down two of the four engines. We touched down in Iceland and the cargo bay erupted in shouts and applause! We trailed behind a "follow-me" truck and stopped at a hardstand. Some guys kissed the ground when they got out of the aircraft. The gauges in the flight deck read zero. I doubt we would have lasted another minute in the air. Suddenly, I had numerous volunteers to help me refuel.

Within an hour we were airborne again and on our way to Goose Bay. Along with the machine gun, we had thrown out numerous pieces of heavy equipment. We tossed globe bars, cuckoo clocks and some cases of oil and hydraulic fluid. Next to go would have been a beautiful grandfather clock. It appeared its time was not yet up!

We flew from Goose Bay on to Texas the next day. The last leg of our trip was uneventful. I didn't think I could have handled much more excitement.

Once back at Dyess, Denise and little Tracy came to the flight line to greet us along with the other wives and families. It was good to be home!

FLIGHT LINE

SEVEN

Last Days at Dyess

I HAD WRITTEN DENISE ABOUT MY NEXT DUTY ASSIGNMENT. I had purposely downplayed it. My new challenge was a one-year assignment to a combat zone and she would not be going.

For a few weeks, we flew training missions on the dirt strip at Dyess. We practiced dropping jeeps and pallets of supplies on the dirt strip. I usually enjoyed watching the pallets slide out from the back of my aircraft. It was dangerous though. A parachute was used sometimes to yank the pallet out. And it did with great force.

Other times we would roll in at low level and pull up at the last minute, letting gravity and our dual rails do the work. Just prior to my time at Dyess, our squadron lost a loadmaster out the back of one of the aircraft as it made a pallet drop. He was not wearing a chute nor was he strapped to the airplane. The young sergeant lost his life in a most unfortunate way.

I ventured close to the open ramp to watch the cargo deploy but not too close as to be another statistic. The loadmasters were enlisted men like myself and were, for the most part, good at their task. The aircraft was mine, but the cargo was theirs. The young loadmasters saw to it that the cargo, whatever it was, was properly loaded, carried and dropped. They were hard workers, and I made many friends among them.

****

After landing one hot afternoon back on the main runway at Dyess, we were met at the airplane by a three-star general dressed in fatigues. He was upset over something the pilot did or didn't do. I stood on the open ramp of my airplane as this general approached. He stopped a few feet away hands on hips, listening to the pilot's excuses. I quickly noticed three white stars on his cap. His left collar had three stars in a row and three more still on his right collar. This guy had nine white stars surrounding his red face! I thought it looked silly. The general asked me a few questions about my C-130. Thankfully, I knew the answers. He was a strong admirer of the Hercules, but clearly not with our pilot on this day. After the general rode off in his staff car, I refueled and started my post-flight inspection. I never saw that particular pilot again. Perhaps he was given a desk job somewhere.

****

As often as I could, I ended my day watching the sunset from the lofty perch above the flight deck. Above the top bunk in the flight deck, was an escape hatch. Crew chiefs used this opening to gain access to the top of the aircraft. It was a nice spot to sit. With my feet dangling inside my flight deck, I had command of my environment. I would just sit for a few moments and observe. The C-130 also had an overhead hatch mid-fuselage and near the tail, but we used them less often.

I flew my last mission on No. 63-7805. This airplane and I had been through a lot together and it was not easy to walk away. I performed my last post-flight inspection and signed off the books. I left a little note for the next crew chief. For the longest time I just stood in the huge empty cargo bay and remembered all the places, all the people and all the situations we had gone through together.

Over the last two years, I had flown hundreds of hours, hauling all kinds of cargo, from a small helicopter and numerous jeeps to a single pallet of frozen steaks. We had moved men and materiel all across this country and Europe. We had rescued people in the Middle East. I had defended this aircraft, using my lock against a communist's rifle. Once, we moved nuclear missiles of some kind and I could not move around my own cargo compartment unless accompanied by another Airman—this was the Air Force's "two-man concept."

We hauled people and livestock, sometimes simultaneously. I saw numerous Army and Marine troops fly out the paratroop doors both in daylight and at night. I was always glad to be staying with my airplane. I enjoyed moving about the entire aircraft during flight, usually checking hydraulics or electronics. I was feeling the pulse of the aircraft that I had come to know inside and out. As anyone who has flown in a C-130 would tell you, riding in the cargo bay was loud. I wore a headset most of the time, both to keep out the noise and to stay in touch with the crew. I kept a long cord to move about. The best ride however, was in the flight deck. I usually would stand behind the pilot and beside the engineer. This way I could see all the important gauges, but I had a commanding view outside. It was considerably quieter up here also. I quite enjoyed the sights from the flight deck windows. All twenty-three of them!

I remember once sipping hot chocolate as we flew high over Norway and its many islands and inlets. It was beautiful and reminded me of home. I had seen much of the world from my flight deck glass and would miss our partnership.

I guess you would almost have to be one to know one, but a crew chief can become attached to his charge. Man and machine. I take care of it and it takes care of me. I had risked my life to protect this one. In return, it moved me safely all about the globe.

Around jets, the smallest loose wire or dropped nut can be ingested into the engines with disastrous results. I kept a tight ship and felt that while certain crews could fly her, she ultimately belonged to me. But not this one...not anymore.

I closed the crew entrance door and shut down the power unit. It was completely quiet as I walked away for the last time. I could hear the "remove before flight" streamers slapping back and forth in the Texas wind. I felt like my trusty C-130 was waving goodbye.

I processed out of the squadron and said goodbye to my friends. My two best friends, John Forsberg and John Rhett, also had orders sending them to the 16th Special Operations Squadron at Ubon, RTAFB in Thailand (were we being "rewarded" for our Amman rescue mission?). I would go over first, followed by Rhett then Forsberg in the following weeks.

It was a special assignment. The squadron of AC-130 gunships consisted of fourteen specially modified aircraft. They were the only aircraft of their kind in the entire world! I remembered the MC-130 combat talon aircraft I had seen at Pope AFB months before. The AC-130 gunships dwarfed even those sophisticated platforms.

Denise, Tracy and I were packed and ready to go, but we couldn't. Our cat had disappeared! We delayed for as long as we could. Some of our friends who had come to see us off promised to watch out for her and if found, send her home to Washington. We started out on our long drive, Denise and Tracy in the station wagon and me driving the Corvette. Just before leaving Abilene, we stopped to top off our fuel. As I was filling up the wagon, I noticed a little black face staring from under a pile of clothes in the back. It was our cat. She had sneaked into the car and hidden under a pile of warm coats. Now at least the whole family would be coming home.

The drive back to Washington was long and tedious. Tracy was teething and kept us up at night. I felt better once we neared Oregon and then Washington. I remembered flying over this area on our way up to Alaska months before. It seemed much longer than that.

We finally made it home and I tried to relax before my departure. Denise and Tracy moved in with her mom. I put my Corvette up on blocks and covered it. The car would be safe in my mom's backyard. We packed some of our belongings into boxes and brought them over to my father-in-law's place in Seattle for safekeeping.

Among the belongings were pictures of my one-thirty, some with the red crosses. While unloading one of the boxes, my father-in-law came up behind me and said, "Hey Tom, I have something for you." I turned around to see him standing five feet away, pointing a pistol at me! A split second later, he fired! Automatically, I staggered backward at the loud report and dropped my hands to feel for the blood that surely was flowing.

There was no blood. He started laughing as he approached me, showing me his new starter's pistol. I was not amused. He didn't know about my close call in Romania and I was not about to tell him. We cut short our visit. I was trembling with anger and wanted to do him bodily harm. Instead, we simply left.

Oddly enough, that was the last time I ever saw him (or our belongings) again. He and his new wife moved out of the area and took our stored items...never to be seen again.

EIGHT

Air Commandos

ALL TOO QUICKLY MY LEAVE WAS OVER, AND MY FAMILY brought me to Sea-Tac Airport in Seattle. It was a tearful goodbye. I flew a commercial jet to San Francisco. From the airport, I caught a taxi with three other military men to Travis AFB. We were all going in the same direction. I found the check-in counter and took my place among the large group of Army, Marine and Air Force personnel headed to Vietnam. I called home to say I had made it this far. When I heard Mom's voice, I got homesick. I hadn't even left the country yet, and I wanted to go home!

We were put on a commercial jet contracted by the U.S. military. We flew to Alaska, refueled and headed to Japan. It was late at night when we touched down at Kadena AFB outside Okinawa. After a short layover, we were airborne again. I had called home again from Japan and felt worse than before. I couldn't shake the feeling that I was not coming back.

Hours later, we touched down at Clark Field in the Philippines. They had rooms available for us just off base. A few of us rode into town in one of the colorful jeep taxies. I had a good steak dinner at the hotel and went to bed. The room was entirely mine, and I felt very much alone.

The next morning, we caught an Air Force C-141 transport to Thailand. The pilot pointed Vietnam out to us as we flew over that war-torn country. It looked peaceful from up above. Sometime later, having overflown Laos as well, we touched down at Ubon Royal Thai Air Force Base, Thailand. As I stepped out of the aircraft, I stepped directly into an oven! I expected it to be hot, but this steaming heat was almost unbearable. I was sweating before I touched the tarmac. This was going to be a long year.

We boarded a bus with wire mesh over the windows. I already knew why the wire was there. I was wondering why *I* was there. We were processed in and met by representatives from the various squadrons. Ubon was home to the 8th Tactical Fighter Wing, known as the Wolf Pack. The 8th, by this time in the war, had a reputation for being the best of the best. The 16th SOS was a squadron under that wing. The 8th TFW flew F-4 Phantoms day and night into North Vietnam.

I was assigned to a hooch near the flight line. A hooch is a tin-roofed structure, similar to a tent with wooden sides. It was just as hot inside as it was outside. I grabbed a cot and put my gear in a locker. I didn't have to report in to the 16th Special Ops duty section until the next day, so I wandered over to the NCO club. I walked in the double front door, passing Airmen coming out...aahh, air conditioning! I ordered a beer. "Maggie May" by Rod Stewart was playing on the jukebox. Two guys I knew from Dyess came over and sat down next to me. I didn't feel so alone anymore. Another sergeant came over to join us. His name was Ed Smith. "Call me Smitty," he said. He grabbed the waitress and ordered another round of beers. I had plenty in my glass and told him, "No thank you."

"Drink it or wear it!" he demanded.

I didn't like this guy. I accepted his free beer but didn't finish it. I didn't want to make waves my first day there. Smitty eventually left our table and joined some others at the bar. "What's with that guy?" I asked.

"He's a gunner with Spectre," someone said.

"Oh shit!" I mumbled.

The next morning I checked in at headquarters of the 16th SOS. I was issued jungle fatigues and jungle boots. At least I would no longer stand out in my Stateside uniform. I walked over to the flight line to catch a glimpse of these Special Operations aircraft. They were both beautiful and ugly at the same time. Each aircraft was painted all black with red prop-tips and bristling with guns. To me, they were ugly because they also had large radomes that housed the gunship's electronics protruding from the fuselage, particularly one on the nose below the pilot's window.

I checked into Squadron Operations. Behind the waste-high counter emerged a silver-haired man. His face and arms were tan and rugged, no doubt from days in the jungle sun. He placed a clipboard on the counter and offered his hand. "Sergeant Combs, welcome to Spectre and the 16th SOS," the chief said. "We've been expecting you."

Taking a copy of my orders the chief scanned them for a moment and said, "Jungle survival school starts in three weeks back in the Philippines. We need IOs and qualified crew chiefs. I'll assign you to an aircraft until we find a permanent position for you. We should know within two weeks what the squadron wants to do with your butt and we'll get your orders processed."

The chief was a senior master sergeant sporting seven stripes. I listened intently to every word. "Alright," he continued, "Staff Sergeant Johnson will be rotating back to the States soon and could use some help, why don't you go introduce yourself." He looked up from his clipboard and added, "Your aircraft is Zero Four Four." I shook his hand firmly again and thanked him for his help.

The Operations chief explained that I could hitch a ride with the line truck to the AC-130. I offered a silent thumbs-up and went back outside into the blistering sun. I found the line maintenance truck and hitched a ride out to where the gunships sat in their revetments.

One gunship I noticed had a large Spectre emblem on the front fuselage. The emblem was a skeleton firing the 20mm guns imposed over a half-moon. Sitting in the back of the van, I noticed a large plastic display indicating each of the squadron's aircraft by number and status. Some of the aircraft had names next to their numbers. No. 623 was *Ghost Rider*; No. 490 was *Thor*; No. 628 was *The Exterminator*; No. 630 was *Azrael-Angel of Death*; and my aircraft, No. 044 (Zero Four Four), was *Prometheus*, the ancient god of fire. I told the driver which one I was looking for, and he took me over to it without hesitating. "Here you are,

Sarge," he announced as we pulled up in front of the revetment. I thanked him for the ride and jumped out the back door. Before me was the giant AC-130 with the red numbers 044 painted above the nose. I had arrived!

I walked up to the crew entrance door on the left side of the fuselage. There was no door! Instead, a large camera and laser designator unit dominated the opening. I walked past the two 20 mm, six-barrel Gatling guns. Behind those and mounted higher up, were two 7.62mm machine guns. I walked between the props of No. 1 and 2 engines and under the left wing. Behind the wheel well of the main landing gear were two 40mm cannons. Further back, behind what was usually the left paratroop door about midway up the fuselage, was the two kilowatt searchlight. The "I" portion of "IO." I reached the ramp at the rear of the aircraft and found a young staff sergeant sitting on the edge. He was writing something in the aircraft's maintenance book.

"Staff Sergeant Johnson?" I asked.

"Yea, that's right," he replied.

"I'm Sgt. Combs and I've been assigned to this aircraft," I said.

"Welcome to Spectre," he responded. He set the logbook on the ramp and gently slid to the ground. He was a tall lanky black man with a broad smile. We shook hands. "Would you like a tour of the airplane?" he inquired.

"Yeah sure," I replied. Together, we jumped up onto the ramp and I got my first glimpse inside the gunship.

Immediately to my right on the ramp was a large square box with numerous tubes protruding from the rear. "This is the flare launcher," he said. He showed me what to avoid so I would not accidentally eject a flare. To my left was the searchlight and forward of that, the two 40mm cannons. They were mounted at an angle pointing downward. Behind the cannons and mounted to the right fuselage just forward of the paratroop door, was an enormous rack filled with 40mm shells. They were in clips of four apiece. Close by were two red fifty-gallon barrels. "For the spent shells," he said pointing to the barrels. "With strong gunners, these forties can fire one hundred rounds per minute."

Halfway down the cargo compartment and slightly off center to the right was a seven-foot wide and fourteen-foot long booth. It reached almost to the ceiling. The entire booth was covered in thick gray flak curtains. There was a door in the center at the back of the booth. We opened it and stepped inside. The booth contained four consoles. Each console had a TV screen which was surrounded with multiple knobs and switches. A high-backed chair faced each monitor. The consoles had a joystick also. The low light level TV console occupied the right rear quadrant of the booth. In the left front was the IR or infrared console. Immediately to its right was what SSgt. Johnson called "Black Crow." "It picks up ignition signals on the ground," he said. The Black Crow console also contained radar homing and warning (RHAW) gear. "This one let's us know when we're being tracked by anti-aircraft artillery or a surface-to-air missile," he said. The last console in the left rear quadrant housed the Fire Control Officer (FCO). Under this console was the bomb damage assessment (BDA) recorder, essentially a videotape machine that recorded what was seen on the screens. By flipping a few switches, each console could view what was being displayed on the other screens. There on the ground and inside the booth, it was as hot as a sauna.

We backed out of the booth and closed the door. Moving to the left, we had just enough room to walk forward and around the booth. Hanging immediately to my left was a long row of parachutes. Directly in front of the booth to the right, was the right scanner's position. In the C-130 I had left behind at Dyess (like all C-130s), this was an emergency exit and was closed at all times. Here on the AC-130 (the "A" in front stood for "Attack"), the exit was open, allowing the right scanner to observe the area below and to the right of the aircraft. Sitting in the scanner's seat, I quickly noticed the prop tips on No. 3 engine were close enough to reach out and grab.

Across the bay, to the left of the scanner's position was an area enclosed in gray flak curtains. Staff Sergeant Johnson opened the curtain to reveal the 7.62mm machine guns. "At high speed," he said, "they'll fire 6,000 rounds per minute." Two fifty-gallon drums were nearby, filled with coiled-up rounds to feed the machine guns. Forward of these guns were the two, 20mm Vulcan Gatling guns, "each capable of firing 2,500 rounds per minute," he told me. A metal plate attached to the side of one of the guns boldly displayed the name and logo of General Electric. Behind the Vulcans was a large wooden "sandbox" with two coal shovels lying nearby. "The gunners shovel the spent shells into these cans," he said, pointing out two more fifty-gallon drums like those in the rear of the aircraft.

At station 245, which was the bulkhead between the cargo area and the flight deck, I found an added rack of sophisticated electronics. "We have manufacture's reps available, to tend to the black boxes," said Johnson. "We don't have to sweat about those. But, we *do* have to keep the aircraft ready to fly...at all times." Some of the boxes had manufacture's labels on them. I noticed Texas Instruments and Singer right away. I thought Singer only made sewing machines. My mind flashed on Nana and all the other grandmothers out there...if they only knew.

We squeezed past the TV camera and laser unit hanging in the doorway and climbed the chest-high stairs to the flight deck. Like the rest of the gunship's interior, the walls were a flat black. Up here it was hot, dark and moody. I noticed the navigator's console spread across the right rear quarter of the deck. It contained Doppler, mapping radar, altimeters, compasses, a Loran C and D computer, gyroscopes, navigation computers, air and ground speed indicators and a host of other panels, switches and dials. There was no room for a bunk! The front portion of the Spectre flight deck was the same as any C-130, except that off to the left of the pilot's seat, was an electronic gun sight. "That's the fire control display," SSgt. Johnson revealed. "It tells the pilot how to maneuver the airplane in order to aim the guns, where the sensors are sighting." The pilot, flight engineer and copilot seats also had armor plates on the sides.

"How many people are on the crew?" I asked.

"Usually thirteen," he replied. "Seven officers and six enlisted."

We climbed back down from the flight deck and made our way back to the ramp. We jumped off the back and started our walk around the outside of the aircraft. Now I understood why the airplane had all these radomes protruding out. They housed the extra electronics that became the eyes and ears of the gunship. Staff Sergeant Johnson identified each of these for me as we walked around the plane. Under each wing, just outboard of the engines, I noticed large tube-like objects. They were painted white. "That's ECM," he said. "Electronic Countermeasures used to jam Charlie's radar." The crew chief wiped his forehead with the back of his hand and grabbed a rag from his pocket as he spoke. "This aircraft is code named 'Surprise Package' because of the armament and avionics."

My new aircraft was an "A" model. It was just like the shiny one I had trained on back at Sheppard AFB a lifetime ago. Looking up, I noticed the large black vertical stabilizer with the red letters "FT" along with the aircraft's serial number below.

"Fucking Tough," He said.

"Huh?" I asked. The crew chief pointed up to the tail. "The red letters, that's what they stand for."

"Oh, yeah," I replied.

"Did you notice the three red stars?" asked Johnson as we walked to the front of the aircraft. "Right there," he said, pointing to the area above the crew entrance door. Sure enough, centered above the laser and camera equipment, a few inches above the opening, were three red stars.

"So...what do they stand for?" I asked. Staff Sergeant Johnson stopped for a moment and got a serious look on his face. "They represent air-to-air kills. This is the only gunship in the squadron to have air-to-air kills. Combined, the squadron air-to-ground kills are in the thousands," Johnson said flatly. "That's done with only twelve gunships. The math is pretty simple."

He continued, "But air-to-air? That's a different story. The only mission I was involved with happened last year. I don't remember which crew it was, but they jumped off the ramp of the gunship whooping and hollering about a North Vietnamese helicopter in flight. The scanner just said, "Target destroyed." The gunship had orbited from above as the enemy helicopter flew at a lower level. "I painted that star myself," Johnson added as he pointed to the far right star. He actually looked quite proud as he boasted of his lineage. "I don't remember the story of the other two stars," he continued, "they were already painted on when I took over almost a year ago. I'll tell you this Sgt. Combs, this gunship has seen some pretty intense combat action. It's a damn fine airplane!"

Staff Sergeant Johnson clearly had great pride in this aircraft. It had been his baby for almost a year. As we walked around the outside of the aircraft he pointed out areas of sheet metal repair. Most, he explained, were from exploding shell fragments. He told me of a few of this craft's exploits, and I grew more amazed with each incident. This was indeed a special group of planes and people.

After a while, I left him with the airplane and walked over to the tool crib. Passing by the squadron's other gunships sitting in the revetments, I noticed the crew chiefs going about their tasks. I felt a tug of pride knowing that at least for now, I would be a part of a special airplane in a squadron of unique and special aircraft.

Opening the door to the tool crib resulted in a blast of cool air. The sergeant in charge had his air conditioner on full tilt. I introduced myself to the chief and showed him my orders. Standing at the counter, I filled out the necessary forms to check out a toolbox. I had to inventory every tool inside and sign off on each piece. Thanking the chief, I knelt down and hoisted the heavy tool box to my shoulder. Spinning around I backed out the door. The immediate feeling was as if I had fallen into an open oven door. The tropical heat was actually shocking when given a taste of air conditioned comfort. The sudden temperature difference was actually nauseating.

I hitched a ride with the line truck again and brought my tools back to the aircraft. I raised the heavy box onto the ramp and dragged it forward of the booth. I found a convenient spot next to the right scanner's position where we would have access to it, but it would be out of the way during flight. (I locked it the next day with the same padlock I had risked my life over, months before in Romania.)

Staff Sergeant Johnson and I started our preflight of the aircraft. I grabbed a hydraulic stand and checked the oil in all four engines. The "A" model was notorious for using up oil. As I walked around on the top of the wing, I quickly noticed that the top surfaces were painted camouflage while the rest of the aircraft was black. I also noticed that virtually every surface was extremely hot to the touch, due to the tropical sun. This high up, I had a commanding view of my surroundings. Ubon was positioned in the middle of the jungle. There was a small village just outside the main gate. "The main town of Ubon is a few miles down the dirt road," shouted Johnson from below. Here on the flight line, besides having the revetments to protect the aircraft, there were coils of barbed wire and guard towers. I noticed the stern look on the face of the guard in the nearest tower. What did he know that I didn't?

"What's with all the security?" I asked SSgt. Johnson when I was back on the ground. "Sappers and snipers," he said.

This was late October 1971 and most ground troops had left Vietnam. President Nixon's "Vietnamization" program was being implemented. This put extra emphasis on American air power to fill the gaps. This fact was not lost to the North Vietnamese. They had increased their attacks on bases in South Vietnam and surrounding areas including Thailand.

"We had a sapper attack three months ago," said SSgt. Johnson. "The Air Police killed one and captured two, right over there," he added, pointing across the runway. "They'll be back. Charlie gets a big reward if he can bag a gunship."

I had been warned already during orientation not to show any military rank or squadron affiliation when off base. The NVA and VC had put a price on our heads. Anyone with knowledge of our gunship's weapons systems or countermeasures would be of great value to them. A VC or even a Thai citizen sympathetic to their cause would be rewarded if we "disappeared." I decided right then to always wear civilian clothes when I left the base.

"What about snipers?" I asked him.

"With all the noise here on the flight line, you can never tell if they are shooting at you or not," he said. "Just be careful when you're on top of the airplane. It's worse at night, when you're silhouetted against the night sky."

Staff Sergeant Johnson then stepped around a B-1 stand and moved to the back of the plane. "With these lights," he continued, pointing to the high-powered lights around our revetments, "we're all targets."

As I was absorbing all this information, the crew bus pulled up behind our aircraft, and the flight crew emerged from the door. Wow! These guys looked ready for a fight! They had their flight suits with flak vests on and their pistol belts hanging off their hips like gunslingers. They carried helmets, and each man was equipped with radios, flares and a survival knife.

I introduced myself to the crew and they welcomed me to Spectre. The pilot did a walk-around the aircraft and asked a few questions. I had questions I wanted to ask him, but I said nothing other than answering his inquiries about the aircraft.

Before long, I was on interphone standing in front of the aircraft. Staff Sergeant Johnson thought I should jump in with both feet, so he suggested I run engine start procedures. "Are we clear to start No. 3?" asked the pilot.

"No. 3 is clear," I said.

"Starting No. 3," he replied. The familiar sound of the T-56 turboprop engine came to life as No. 3 prop started spinning. I moved to my right, pulling the large fire extinguisher behind me as I went. If a fire erupted on engine start-up, I was to rush forward and hose it down with the fire extinguisher, avoiding the props. So far, I had never had to use it. From my position out front, I could no longer see the rest of the crew as they got ready. I could only see the pilot, copilot and engineer as they ran through the checklist for engine start. Their helmeted heads were turning and twisting in the dimly lit flight deck. I watched the pilot closely, waiting for his look in my direction. Over the intercom I could hear the other crewmembers as they checked in to their positions. Off to one side, I heard another AC-130 starting engines. The sound was muffled both by my headset and the large revetment wall between us. On 044 the pilot turned his head toward me but said nothing. I could see the ailerons and elevators moving as the pilot checked hydraulics and flight controls. Finally, he looked over at me and nodded his head.

"Ready to start No. 2 chief," came the pilot's voice over my headphones.

"No 2. is clear," I responded quickly.

"Starting No. 2," he said.

With both inboard engines running, I pulled the extinguisher off to the side of the revetment. Next, I moved to the ground power unit to switch it off. I pulled the big heavy black cable from the receptacle just below the pilot's window and coiled it on top of the power unit. I attached the hinged Black Crow fairing to the fuselage. This large front radome required its own fairing for stability. Then, I moved the power unit off to the side and walked directly in front of the airplane. We would start the other two engines and arm the weapons once we were away from the revetment. I stood maybe twenty feet off the nose of the aircraft and waited for the pilot's signal. I looked at this huge black monster with "044" painted in red on the nose and guns hanging off the side. I was filled with a sense of awe and excitement. I remembered the MC-130 Combat Talons back at Pope AFB. I wouldn't trade with those guys now for anything!

The pilot gave me the thumbs-up signal. We couldn't talk to each other now because I had disconnected my interphone at the same time I had pulled away the power unit. I raised my hands and motioned thumbs out. This told SSgt. Johnson we were ready to pull the big wooden chocks between the tires. He ran around both sides of the airplane from behind, pulling at the chocks by their thick ropes. I motioned the pilot to come forward. He moved slowly, the gunship's nose dipping down then up, as he tested his brakes. Once clear of the revetment, I signaled a right turn. As he started his turn to line up on the taxiway, I moved out of the way to avoid the spinning prop.

"Good job, Sarge," said Johnson. I flipped him the thumbs up. I knew Johnson was testing me. He wanted to know if I had what it takes. I was ready. We jumped into the line truck and followed the gunship down the taxiway past the other AC-130s. Some of those gunships were ready to taxi now as well.

Near the runway and away from the revetments now, I plugged into the gunship's intercom again and stood by another fire extinguisher. Speaking on headset, I cleared the pilot as he started first one then the other outboard engine. I pulled the extinguisher off to the side on the grass and approached the front of the aircraft again. The pilot was radioing the tower for take-off clearance. He gave me the nod of his helmet and I snapped to attention and held a salute. He saluted back and flashed me a quick thumbs up. "Chief, Spectre two-zero is ready," the pilot said, indicating tonight's call sign. "Roger." I replied.

Running up to the open crew entrance door, I unplugged my intercom, pulling the long cord with me. I moved off to the side and let the aircraft pass by. As they were moving away from me and towards the runway, I could see the gunners moving things around behind the booth. The ramp was up but the door was open. This is how they would fly and fight.

I walked back to the line truck and jumped inside. We watched the airplane take off into the now darkening sky. We passed the other gunships moving out as we headed back to the maintenance shack. "It looks like you've done this before Sarge," said SSgt. Johnson as we got out of the truck. He slapped me on the back. "You'll do just fine!" He said. I had been accepted. I was Spectre. I was "Sierra Hotel" (shit hot).

We decided on a quick meal at the flight line snack bar. Soon we were joined by other crew chiefs that had also seen their airplanes off. Sitting around the picnic table, Johnson introduced me to the others. "How long will they stay out?" I asked one crew chief. "Usually about four hours," he said. "Sometimes they'll stay a little longer. It depends on what they find and where they go."

Spectre's mission was to interdict the Ho Chi Minh Trail, which was the main supply route that linked North Vietnam to South Vietnam. The trail ran primarily through Laos and to a lesser extent, Cambodia. "They're diverted for TIC Missions as well," Johnson added. "That's Troops in Contact," another chief said. "If a group of friendlies are being overrun, they'll call Spectre to come to their rescue," added another. "It keeps us busy," Johnson said.

I asked "So, what do we do now?"

"Well," said one, "we can go help some of the other crew chiefs whose planes are not flying tonight, or we can hang out in the crew chiefs' lounge."

"What's the crew chiefs' lounge?" I asked.

"Come on, I'll show you," SSgt. Johnson said, grabbing my sleeve.

We left the others at the snack bar and walked out to the flight line. It was getting dark by now and the huge floodlights were switched on. The seven remaining AC-130s not yet flying that night sat in their revetments, tended to by their respective crew chiefs. Johnson and I headed towards the left side of one long row of revetments. Around the side and towards the back of the revetment, was a trailer parked on the grass. We approached the trailer and opened the door. Inside were a handful of chairs and a card table. "This," he said, "is the crew chief 's lounge. It's a good idea not to wander too far away while your airplane is flying, you never know when something can come up and the aircraft returns early. You're expected to be here."

I was not in the mood to sit inside the small 8-by-12 trailer, so I told SSgt. Johnson that I was going to check out the other aircraft. "Be careful," he warned "or they'll put you to work." I nodded and walked outside. I started up the row of revetments and quickly noticed not all the gunships were the older "A" model like mine. Some were the newer "E" model with four-bladed props like those I had left behind at Dyess. I stopped at a couple of them and talked with their crew chiefs. Sure enough, I ended up assisting them with a few tasks.

I stopped at one gunship to admire the nose art painted below the pilot's side window. I introduced myself and told the crew chief which aircraft I had been assigned to. "Johnson's?" he asked. "Yeah," I said, "Zero Four Four."

"Watch out for Staff Sergeant Wilson on oh-four-three; that guy's crazy," he said. "He threatened to blow up his airplane."

"What?" I asked, not understanding.

"Yeah, he was tired of all the killing last dry season and made some threats." he said. "They sent him to see the shrink and took him off the line for a while."

I shook my head in disbelief.

"He's mellowed since then," he continued, "but be careful and keep your eyes open." I said I would and told the chief I'd see him around.

"Where in the world are you from?" he asked as I was leaving.

"Seattle."

"Really?"

"Yeah," I said, "and you?"

"I'm from Dallas, Texas," he said proudly.

I wandered around for a while longer then headed back to the flight line snack bar. Now with the lights on, I saw a big sign above the door of the squadron maintenance shed. It read, "16th SOS Fabulous Four Engine Fighters."

Another line truck pulled up alongside the building and the driver said flatly, "Some of them are on their way back."

"Okay," I said.

"Hop in," he said, "I'll give you a ride."

I got into the van and we headed towards the flight line. Located behind us in this van like the other line truck, was a young staff sergeant sitting before the large status board. The board had listed by serial number, each of the 14 AC-130s and their daily status. On the far right column of two of them, the letters "BD" were in red. "What's that?" I asked pointing to one of them. "Battle damage," he responded.

I was accustomed to grounding my aircraft because of engine problems, fuel problems or a hydraulic leak; however, battle damage was completely new.

We stopped in front of the crew chiefs' lounge and a few guys, including SSgt. Johnson, came out and jumped into the truck. We rode to the aircraft recovery area just off the main runway and waited for the gunships to land. Aircraft No. 569 was the first to land, followed by No. 043, then No. 044. Staff Sergeant Johnson and I got out of the van, and I grabbed a pair of wands. These were flashlights with long orange extensions at the tip. They allowed the pilot to see me in the dark.

I was positioned near our revetment when the gunship came around the corner. It had shut down the two outboard engines and had its running lights switched on. I stood in front of the revetment and held my hands straight up holding a wand in each hand. I motioned the aircraft forward and indicated left or right with the wands, trying to keep the nose gear on a yellow line. With an aircraft the size of a C-130 bearing down on you, most anyone would instinctively dive for cover, running to one side or another. This would be the case especially at night. I had by now grown accustomed to having a huge C-130 heading straight towards me, engines roaring, blades slicing. Hell, I'm actually inviting him *in*…with the movement of the wands!

Finally, when the aircraft was a little past our revetment, I signaled with a crossing of the wands for it to stop. The props became visible as the pilot shut down engines. Staff Sergeant Johnson ran behind the aircraft and put chocks down between the tires. A crew bus pulled up alongside the gunship. As the crew jumped down off the lowered ramp at the back of the aircraft, I noticed some were sullen and quiet, while others were boisterous and talking loudly.

"That had to be a fuel truck," one was saying, "for it to blow like that. Man what else could it have been?"

"Maybe they just used a higher octane fuel," one of the gunners joked. The pilot jumped down and walked over to where SSgt. Johnson and I were standing. "A good airplane, Sarge," he said. "I've got no complaints at all." The flight engineer handed me the logbook. He had written a few minor discrepancies in the book, but nothing serious. They piled into the crew bus and headed to Operations for debriefing.

I wheeled the ground power unit up and connected electrical power. We started our post-flight inspection. I took oil samples from each engine. This was for the engine lab to test for metal content. I jumped down when the fuel truck arrived and assisted Johnson as he pumped JP-4 jet fuel back into the tanks. Within an hour or so, a tug showed up and we connected the long bar to the nose wheel. I went up to the flight deck and sat in the pilot's seat, manning the brakes.

We slowly pushed the aircraft back into its revetment. Stepping down from the flight deck, I noticed the fifty-gallon drums inside the aircraft were all full of spent ammo. I reached down and picked up a single 20mm shell casing. It was still warm.

A blue pick-up truck pulling a trailer came alongside the gunship. Two guys jumped out and approached us. They were here to remove the spent shells and provide us with new rounds of ammo. The smell of cordite filled the cargo bay. I wondered where the crew had gone and what they had shot at. I fingered the 20mm casing in my pocket. I wondered if the other half of this had killed someone tonight. Once finished, we covered the intakes and put "remove before flight" streamers in place. I shut down the power unit and we headed for the barracks. It was close to 4:30 in the morning and I was tired. I slept well until the sun came up, then it became too hot. I stayed in bed but didn't get much sleep.

Around 10:00 a.m., I got up and went to the NCO club for breakfast. I walked inside and immediately felt the cool, air-conditioned air. "Maggie May" by Rod Stewart, was playing *again* on the jukebox. I wondered what the day would bring.

After eating, I stayed awhile just to enjoy the coolness. Then I ventured out and went down to the post office to get a box assigned to my name. I now had an address.

I went to the base library (also air-conditioned) and fired off a quick letter home. I wandered around the base a while to get the lay of the land. I had decided already that I needed a black Spectre hat like everyone else in my squadron seemed to be wearing. The Thai Tailor Shop, which was located next to the barbershop, provided one for just two dollars. I had my name and home state printed on it, along with the dates 1971-1972.

As I walked into the maintenance building one of the line chiefs mentioned they were about to start a meeting and I should be there. Grabbing a coffee at the doorway, I followed him into the room and sat down. The chief of maintenance was talking about the upcoming season.

"Gentlemen," he started. "The dry season officially starts November 1st and will run until May of next year. We will be operating in the Steel Tiger area of Laos. Intelligence tells us Charlie has moved more guns into the area, so we will expect battle damage. It's your job to keep 'em flying and fighting. November officially kicks-off Operation Commando Hunt Seven. I expect you to do your jobs as you've been trained to do. Some of you will be rotating back to the World soon. Let's make good use of this time to get the new members up to speed." Others in the room began to yell, "Short! Short!"

"This year," he said, "we'll continue to reward the ground crew having the highest truck kills with two cases of beer each month." More shouts of "Right on," "All right" and "Shit hot," came from the group. "Do your jobs and keep them in the air." he said. He introduced a few new members of the squadron including me and asked the others to give us new guys their support and benefit of experience.

After the meeting, a few guys came up to me and introduced themselves and offered their assistance. I told them I appreciated that. One of them asked me where I was staying. I pointed in the direction of the hooch not far from the flight line. "Oh, that's no good," he said. "When I leave, you can have my place in the new barracks." He told me they were at the opposite end of the base and away from the flight line. "It's not quite as noisy there and," he continued, "they're air-conditioned!"

"Wow, that's great," I told him. "I accept."

Staff Sergeant Johnson and I grabbed a ride with the line truck and headed out to our aircraft for preflight. We also had time to take care of some of those minor write-ups given to us by the flight engineer the day before.

As dusk rolled in, the crew buses began showing up in front of the airplanes. We got the same crew as yesterday. I walked around the aircraft with the pilot as he was kicking the tires and looking around for fluid leaks. He asked me where I was previously stationed. I told him Dyess in Abilene, Texas.

"Great place," he said. "I was there myself about two years ago." We had something in common. I asked him a few questions about their missions over here. "For every one we take out," he said, "Charlie seems to come up with two to replace 'em."

I told him I was offered a choice between IO and crew chief. "Are you married?" he asked. "Yes, sir," I said, "with a one-year-old daughter."

"Both positions are extremely important," he said. "I would talk to some of the other IOs to get their perspective."

Our conversation was interrupted when the navigator came running up from behind the airplane. Apparently, it was an urgent matter. The young captain said he needed to talk to the pilot. "Thank you, sir," I said as we parted.

Before long I was standing in front of the aircraft and responding to the pilot's questions. "Chief we clear to start No. 3?"

"No. 3 is clear," I answered. We went through the same sequence as the night before. I offered a crisp salute to the pilot who this time gave me a broad smile along with his thumbs up. Once the aircraft had taken off, SSgt. Johnson and I rode back to the snack bar and waited for the other crew chiefs to join us.

One thing I had noticed after arriving here at Ubon was the constant level of noise. The primary source of that noise was the 433rd and 435th squadrons of Phantom jets. They usually took off in pairs. Two would lift off, then two more, then two more still. It seemed to be never ending.

The sight and sound of the F-4s retracting their landing gear as they soared past us in full afterburners, was awesome! Sometimes the pilots would look over at us and give us the thumbs up as they took off. These pilots were heading north, to face the most heavily defended areas of Hanoi or Haiphong. Their primary mission was to special areas in North Vietnam, taking out power plants and bridges, etc. They also hunted MIGs. A more recent role was that of flying escort for our gunships. We could use our laser unit to lock onto an anti-aircraft gun and the F-4 would place a laser guided missile on the gun, with effective results. Or they would orbit higher than the gunship and watch for the guns firing on it. Then they would swoop down on the enemy with guns, missiles or napalm.

I began to notice fewer F-4s returning to base than had left. The squadron had its own newspaper called the *Phantom Flyer,* and it usually contained information about this pilot or that pilot who had not returned. Of course, some pilots diverted to another base due to fuel needs or battle damage. They would show up a day or two later with a story. However, some brave aircrews did not return at all.

****

Behind our revetments and past the barbed wire was the main runway itself. This provided us with front row seats to the action. It seemed as if every day a Phantom or two would return with battle damage and the fire trucks would race out to the runway to standby. We could emerge through the hatch on top of our 130s, walk out on a wing and gain a perfect view of the emergency landings.

The emergencies were not always just outside our revetments either. As an armament crew delivered and loaded ammo into our gunship one morning, one of the guys shouted, "Oh shit…" a split second before we all heard and felt the loud clang and bang of two racks of 40mm shells hitting the aircraft floor. Some spilled out through the right paratroop door and crashed to the pavement below. The loader was carrying too much at once and they slipped out of his grasp. I don't know if they would have gone off or not but anything was possible. With this mixture of jet fuel and ammunition on board there wouldn't be much left of us to send home. We all froze momentarily, waiting for the explosion. Then as we all began breathing again, each of us shouted various obscenities to the loader. My feeling is we were all very lucky that day.

One afternoon, I was having a meal at the NCO club when a group of IOs came over and sat down. It was Halloween back in the States. "Maggie May" was playing again on the jukebox. I started asking questions about the job of IO.

"We don't operate the searchlight anymore," one stated, "because the unit is computerized now and operated from the booth."

"Yeah," said another, "our job is rear scanner."

They went on to tell me all about the rear scanner position. With the cargo ramp up and the cargo door open, the scanner lay on the ramp looking back and below pointing out Triple A (anti-aircraft artillery). Tethered with a cable to the gunship, the scanner could literally hang out of the rear of the plane. "Oh, we'll kick out a few flares occasionally," one said, "but the real illumination is what's coming up at us. If it's accurate, we inform the pilot who rolls out of orbit and hopefully avoids a hit." They told me about the different types of Triple-A that I could expect to see. They explained the differences between the orange bursts of 37mm and the bright white of 57mm. It was not unusual, I was told, for the rear scanner to actually fall out of the aircraft during violent maneuvers! Usually one of the gunners would stop loading the 40mm long enough to walk to the ramp and pull him back inside. The IOs tether was all that kept him with the airplane!

The Spectre gunship searches the night, her sensors alert to the enemy.

Once it finds its target, the gunship moves into a 30-degree angle of left bank and begins circling high above, bringing its weapons to bear on the enemy targets below. This method, provided the enemy with a predictable flight path. The plane flew usually only at night and without any lights, so it is by sound rather than sight that the enemy gunners would fire. They had a few years' practice by now and were getting better. I was told some enemy guns were guided by radar as well.

It was clear to me that these guys loved their job. They felt invincible and wouldn't have it any other way. They all felt I should "go for it" and become one of them. I must admit I did not share their enthusiasm. I was invited up to the "gunners' hooch" later to play poker. The Spectre gunners and scanners shared a common barracks. Because they flew at night and rested during the day, their barracks windows were covered over with foil. When I stopped by to play poker, I noticed right away the eerie feel of the darkened room. These guys were nocturnal and preferred the dark. Stepping out from the barracks was like coming out of a movie theater during the day. The heat and bright sun were oppressive. I began to enjoy the "atmosphere" of the scanners barracks.

****

We were into the second week of November 1971, and by then I had procedures down. It was exceptionally hot and humid the night of Saturday the13th. Johnson and I launched our aircraft, only this time with a different crew. These guys were rowdy and loud, even some of the officers. They were going to "get some" according to one of the gunners. The rear scanner was one of the guys I had met and talked with in the NCO club a few weeks prior.

I did a walk-around with the pilot, Captain Baertle, and addressed his concerns about specific areas of the aircraft. The captain was a replacement pilot with this particular crew. This crew's AC was too sick to fly tonight. Consequently the captain and I spent extra time going over the gunship's logbook. He needed to know what kind of ship he'd be flying. The aircrews usually rotated among the gunships for their missions, so they rarely got to know any one gunship closely, unless by circumstance. Once the pilot and I finished and the crew was on board, I moved to the front of the aircraft. I plugged in the interphone cord and began engine start-up. "Ready to start No. 3," said the AC. "No. 3 is clear," I answered. I had no way to know at the time, but we were starting this No.3 engine for the last time ever!

After starting No. 2 engine, I pulled the fire bottle over to the side. "Ready to taxi chief," said the pilot. "Roger," I replied as I coiled up the intercom line. I unplugged myself from the aircraft and moved away from her deadly props. We followed the gunship to the arming area and started the remaining two engines. I gave the pilot a crisp salute and thumbs up. He returned both and taxied away. I waved to the camera, knowing they were switched on and being tested. I noticed the scanner in back and waved to him. He gave me thumbs up in return. I watched as my gunship roared away into the darkness just five minutes after midnight. Soon, all I could see was a red glow from her open rear door. It rose higher as it slowly grew smaller. It looked like Triple-A in slow motion. We jumped into the line truck and sped away.

A couple hours later, SSgt. Johnson and I were sitting in the crew chiefs' lounge when the line truck came to a screeching stop right outside the door. Sergeant Jarvis, a guy I had known back at Dyess, poked his head in the doorway and asked, "Zero Four Four?"

"Right here," I answered.

"Come with me," was all he said as he disappeared from the doorway. Johnson and I got up and followed him outside to the waiting truck. Before I could ask, Sgt. Jarvis said, "Your gunship has been hit! It sounds bad. They're trying to make it back to Ubon."

We rode in silence to the recovery area just off the main runway. The fire trucks had already begun to arrive at various positions along the airstrip. An HH-43 helicopter carrying a bucket underneath filled with fire retardant was circling nearby.

Word came over the radio that two of our AC-130s were just a few minutes away. We waited and watched. "There she is!" someone yelled. Two gunships, one high and one low were approaching the far end of the runway. The higher gunship banked to the left and broke away. He had been flying escort. I could see that the landing gear was down, but the nose of my aircraft kept swinging left and right. The gunship hit the runway hard and bounced up again. As it came back down, it veered to the left then back to the right. As it came closer to our position, we could begin to make out some of the damage. Flames erupted from the main wheel wells as the aircraft slowed then performed a ground loop before coming to a stop on the grass next to the runway.

We jumped back into the truck and sped toward the smoking aircraft. The fire truck had already reached the plane and smothered the landing gear with foam. The crewmen were helping each other off the ramp as we arrived. Our driver parked the truck under the left wing. An ambulance pulled alongside.

Some from the crew were sitting on the grass now, away from the aircraft. I walked over to the flight engineer and asked him what happened. "Jesus!" he said, "Oh sweet, Lord Jesus," he repeated. I saw the rear scanner and walked over to him and caught part of his explanation. "We started an orbit around a truck that had its lights on, but before anyone could say 'flak-trap,' we got hit! We were just breaking back out of orbit when it slammed into us! Pearson, man he got it bad!" Pearson was the right scanner.

I moved off to have a look at my aircraft and was stunned at what I saw. No. 3 and No. 4 engines were half gone! There were no props, just a mess of twisted metal with wires and hoses hanging in all directions. I looked at the right side of the fuselage and noticed numerous holes. One of the gunners came up and said, "I think I soiled my pants man; fuck I just don't believe it!" I walked over to where the pilot and copilot were standing. The squadron commander arrived and the crew began to calmly recount what had happened.

They had just started working over some trucks in Steel Tiger East of the Bolovens Plateau (Delta96) and the Triple A had been moderate. The rear scanner had called accurate to some Triple-A at the seven o'clock position. The pilot just broke out of his orbit to the right when they felt a tremendous thud and saw a bright flash. The copilot and engineer immediately checked the instruments, and they showed all systems to be okay. According to the gauges, all four engines were still running! The flight engineer raced back to the right scanner's position. They had received a 37mm hit just behind No. 4 engine's propeller. The explosion separated the props from the engine. Shrapnel and the engines' prop assembly then smashed into No. 3 engine and also caused its props to spin off. The first explosion and shrapnel knocked the right scanner clear across the airplane and into the flak curtains. He was hurt, but because he was down on the floor he missed the second lethal volley of shrapnel, which was centered on his window. Parts from No. 3 engine's prop and gearbox assembly had peppered the entire area around the scanner's opening.

Despite what the gauges in the cockpit read, the gunship was kept in the air only by the two engines on the left wing. They were about a half-hour flying time from Ubon. The crew decided to coax the aircraft back. The gunners jettisoned all loose equipment to lighten the load. The IO also suggested they jettison the ammo, and the pilot agreed. The gunners started stringing the belts of 20mm out the back of the aircraft wanting to see how far they could make their stream, when static electricity started to cook off some of the rounds. That put a quick end to their play. Instead they started dropping clips of 40mm rounds attached to flares to "bomb" Charlie on the way home. The gunship could not regain altitude so they had to fly around the mountain range.

About ten minutes out, Capt. Baertle noticed the two remaining engines were over-torqueing and overheating. The crew prepared to bail out. They lowered the landing gear, and thankfully had no problems with that. Since he could not use engine reverse thrust to slow down, the pilot relied completely on the brakes to bring the aircraft to a stop. It was the overheated brakes that caused the fire we had seen.

After a tug showed up, I hitched the tow bar to the nose wheel, and we cleared everyone away so we could get the aircraft away from the runway. It was quite a chore getting the huge gunship off the soft grass. Once free of the shoulder and back on the runway, I was tasked with "riding the brakes." This simply meant I was to sit inside the flight-deck in the pilot's seat, and upon some malfunction with the tow bar or the tug pulling us, I was to press both rudder pedals forward to apply the aircraft brakes. Usually we would be running the GTC to provide power for lights and hydraulics. Tonight we had to run dark with no power.

I jumped on board from the lowered ramp and by memory weaved my way forward past the guns and the sensors' booth to the flight deck stairs. Passing by the booth my boots were sticking on the floor. I flashed on the thought that some hydraulic fluid had been spilled. I continued forward in total darkness to the flight deck stairs. Outside lights provided me some illumination once I reached the flight deck. Now, sitting in the semi-darkened flight deck of Zero Four Four, I had no power, no lights and certainly no brakes. I was of little value up there other than following the checklist and doing things by the book; this provided me with the luxury of reenactment. It was just minutes earlier that this very aircraft was hit by anti-aircraft artillery and by miracle and fortitude arrived home intact....mostly. I could "feel" the vibration of the nights' events...as if I were there. Of course hearing what happened from the crewmen I had by now a vivid account of the action. But now, sitting alone in the very same flight deck that moments ago emanated with danger, confusion and life saving decisions in the middle of battle, I was awe-struck. It was...spiritual. I don't think I am able to explain the amazing feelings coursing through my body at this time. Looking out the side windows from the darkened flight deck, I could see ground crews stop in mid-sentence and stare as we slowly passed by.

After a while we had it backed into our revetment and under the lights. Getting up from the pilot's seat, I made my way back through the gunship in complete darkness. I walked right into the 40mm gun, banging my elbow in the process. I jumped off the ramp and started to walk around my aircraft. Now, under the lights, I could see the full extent of the damage. I was absolutely amazed that this aircraft had been damaged so severely, yet flew back and landed safely. I climbed the stairs of a raised B-1 stand and jumped on the left wing. I walked the length of the fuselage and back. I noticed the leading edge of the right wing was completely peppered with shrapnel and showed signs of being twisted. The two engines also bore signs of being twisted on their mounts. Panels of airplane skin were wrinkled in waves. Miraculously, what was left of No. 3 and 4 engines stayed attached to the wing. That the wing itself had stayed on was no less than a miracle.

This was mute testimony to the durability of the C-130 aircraft. Not to mention the ability and the bravery of her crew.

Staff Sergeant Johnson brought up a power cart and started the process to bring power and lights to the damaged airplane. Someone called my name from down below, so I jumped back down onto the stand and quickly moved down the steep angled stairs. Once on the ground I walked to the back of the gunship. "You won't believe it inside now," said SSgt. Johnson as he jumped off the ramp.

I entered the aircraft from the ramp again and slowly walked forward. The flare launcher was gone! So were the fifty-gallon barrels of spent shells. I missed that the first time through. I moved around the two 40mm guns and past the booth. There was blood everywhere! I almost choked. The side scanner's position had numerous holes around the opening. My toolbox below the scanner seat was covered with blood. The floor was streaks of red interrupted by boot prints. There was a small pool of blood near the flak curtains where the scanner had lain.

"Sergeant Combs?" someone was calling from the back of the aircraft. I turned around from where I had stomped through minutes before in the darkness, and choosing my steps to avoid the blood, headed back outside. It was the line chief. "We are not to touch anything until the investigators go over it."

"Yes, sir!" I replied.

"And Combs," he added, "I'll need you on this aircraft as a crew chief."

I wrote my name in the 781 form in the aircraft flight deck. My first task as a crew chief was to put a red X in the book and ground my new charge! I wrote "battle damage, No.3 and No.4 engines including right wing area" and signed my name. Staff Sergeant Johnson was happy to turn over his aircraft to me as well. He was "short" and would be rotating back to the World within a few days.

As a Spectre crew chief, I had access to and control over one of the most lethal weapons of the Vietnam War. This was an awesome responsibility.

For the next day and a half, it seemed the entire population of Ubon paraded past my aircraft. Most people just looked at the damage and shook their heads.

I had been given the okay to clean up the right scanner's area of blood. Now, on my hands and knees scrubbing up the dried blood, I laughed inside at my recoil only a short day ago. I was now in the process of scraping up dried blood from all over the floor, the flak curtains and various racks of equipment. When I opened my toolbox, I discovered blood on some of the tools inside as well. With a sense of adventure, I began a journal and kept the notebook in the box.

One of the squadrons' navigators told me one evening about another gunship that had been hit. He said it limped back to base two years earlier with severe battle damage, only to crash land at Ubon. Two of her crewmembers died. One was the IO. We were more fortunate this time: Sgt. Pearson would live, but he would not return to fly for some time.

Someone came out to the airplane with a Polaroid camera and took a small library of pictures. I grabbed a couple and sent them home in a letter.

We began to remove all the panels in the wing area to fully assess the damage. It was clear that 044 would be out of commission for a while. The pressure was on us to get it repaired and back into the air again.

****

I was up on the wing a couple of days after the incident, removing a fuel dry bay panel, when I heard the firetruck sirens. I stopped working and watched as an F-4 Phantom came in trailing smoke. The runway had arresting barriers set up, much like those on an aircraft carrier. He missed the first barrier and plowed into the second one. Fire engulfed the jet as the pilot and his back-seater jumped or fell out of the cockpit. They both got up and ran to the side of the runway and away from the flames.

****

While early repairs were underway on the gunship, life was about to get better. John Rhett finally arrived from the States. Right away he was put into the new air- conditioned barracks that I had been waiting weeks to get into. The bunk below his was empty, so I grabbed my gear and moved in with John. Later that day the line truck stopped just outside the revetment. I was up on my wing and noticed John jumping out of the back of the truck. He slapped the side of the blue Ford like a cowboy sending his horse on its way. Moments later as he stood in the shadow of my damaged right wing, John shouted up that he had been assigned to Zero Four Four. Perfect!

It was decided we should tow the aircraft to a revetment closer to the maintenance buildings. On this trip across the tarmac, we were a like a giant black bird with a broken wing. Right away I noticed again how everyone working in the revetments had stopped and turned to look at us. This time as we slowly passed by the other gunships, with our hoses and wires hanging beside twisted metal, the ground crews were saluting us!

Once in the new revetment, we began in earnest to repair the gunship. All four engines were removed. We replaced the main landing gear wheels, tires and brakes. Enough damage had been done to the right wing to require its complete removal.

The C-130 carries most of it fuel in the wings. Each wing has a number of fuel tanks, each separated by a fuel dry bay. This small section housed the fuel pumps and numerous other electronics. It was about the size of a phone booth on its side. In the gunships, the dry bays were filled with blocks of foam to help absorb fuel in case of enemy hits in the wings. I pulled all the foam from the right wing dry bays and stored it in the aft cargo area by the 40mm guns. A pile of foam soon became a nest for bees. No doubt, they were drawn to the foam by the sweet fragrance of jet fuel. While we waited for a wing replacement to arrive from the States, I battled with the bees in my cargo area.

Working in and around the gunship at night, we used the red combat lighting to work by. It breathed a strong sense of nocturnal combat from this perspective. Actually I enjoyed working by the red glow. Not every task could be done in the soft light of course, so we would switch to white light when necessary. Sometimes, late at night I would sit in the flight deck at the navigator's table writing a letter home. Many letters were born in the soft red glow of my gunship's flight deck amid the hum of avionics and ground power units. Outside, F-4s or our squadron's gunships would be landing or taking off into the night sky. The flight line was in constant motion day and night.

We placed jacks under the left wing, so when the right wing was detached the plane would not roll over. It required immense effort to disassemble and remove the wing components. Others in our squadron helped with this daunting task. A crane was brought in and used to pull off the battle-damaged wing. Days later, a new wing arrived, and we began the huge task of attaching it and all its associated hardware. I spent a few days patching the holes in the fuselage and spot painting them black. We watched each evening as the other crew chiefs readied their aircraft then launched them into the night sky. December came. We didn't get the two cases of beer for November's truck kills.

The pressure was on to keep the squadron's aircraft in the air. Some could handle the pressure and some could not. Staff Sergeant Johnson had rotated home, so it was up to John and me to get our gunship back into fighting form. We now had the new wing attached and were waiting for our new engines to be flown in from the States. Once in a while, John and I would leave our aircraft and help launch or recover some of the others. More often, the others were over helping us rebuild our ship.

For the second time since the gunship was damaged, another friend came to Ubon. John Forsberg arrived from the States. It was good to see him again. Right away we filled him in. His first night in-country, I proudly showed him my gunship as it sat to one side in the dark. With no engines and a different colored right wing it looked odd. John was sympathetic and supportive. He said he wanted to be assigned to Zero-Four-Four, if they would let him. John Rhett suggested we find a place in our barracks for Sgt. Forsberg. I thought it was a great idea, only there was no room left in our barracks. So, John was assigned to a room down the street. It turned out he was assigned to a different aircraft also.

****

Often we played poker with the gunners and scanners in their barracks located next to ours. Occasionally flares would go off around the base perimeter and the Air Police would race to the scene. We'd stop our game long enough to see what was going on. Then with a yawn, we'd head back to our room. Sometimes if the game was intense enough we would ignore the flares. We figured if we didn't hear gunfire or explosions, then all was well.

I had been here for seven weeks and had not once left the base. Finally one day, my friends and I ventured into the little town just outside the main gate. We enjoyed a great kobi steak and a rub-n-scrub in the bathhouse on the corner. The Thai girls were looking cuter as the weeks went by. We picked them by a little red number on their "uniform." The girls sat behind a large glass window. They chatted among themselves or watched television, while we decided which one or two we wanted.

If they spoke some English, that would be a bonus. Of course, the only way to find out was to choose one. They worked very hard to soothe our anxieties. Over time, we tried a few different bathhouses then found our favorite. A massage cost about forty Baht; two dollars!

We usually spent off duty time at the base BX planning our stereo purchases. The BX specialized in stereo gear and cameras. The prices were just too good to pass up.

The base had a theater also which played old movies and helped to make us feel at home. For a dollar I could see a movie, eat a bag of popcorn and drink a can of pop or beer.

Back on the flight line we continued to put Zero Four Four back together. Even small tasks were made difficult, because of the intense heat. It was like working on a stove without the burner being shut off first. We wore gloves most of the time but still I burned my hands on numerous occasions. Sergeant Rhett and I were now "officially" Bent Nail Qualified. This was a patch bestowed upon any crew chief having to repair battle damage. John and I were given these patches one day by the line chief who also provided two Battle Damage Qualified patches as well. We both stuck them in our pockets and went back to work.

At the end of our day we would cool our parched throats and hands with a cool beer or soda at the NCO club. Late one night, I noticed a particularly loud and obnoxious group in one corner of the club. Someone was shouting, "I don't care anymore, I don't care!" One guy from their group walked past us and said, "Oh excuse my buddy, he's an F-4 crew chief. His jet was shot down, no chutes!" The chief was drenching himself now with a pitcher of beer and becoming unruly. He was a mess! We left the club and returned to the barracks. Usually Rhett and I would put on headphones and crank up our stereo. We could groove to the music and forget for a while where we were. Sign of the times: my favorite song was "Melancholy Man" by the Moody Blues. The F-4 crew chief would dry out and return to the flight line. He would be assigned to a replacement aircraft. And the war continued.

****

KABOOM! John and I looked at each other as we sat on the ramp of our aircraft. "What the hell was that?" John asked. "It came from the revetment next to us," I said.

The two of us jumped down and ran around the revetment wall to see what had caused the explosion. Lying on the ground was one of the senior crew chiefs. He had his aircraft's flare pistol in his right hand. The top of his head was gone! He wasn't moving. People from all directions came running to the area. As we moved closer, the line trunk pulled up and a couple of guys jumped out. "What happened?" One of them asked. "I don't know," John replied. "We heard the explosion and ran over and found him like this."

A small crowd continued to gather as an ambulance pulled up next to us. Someone put a towel over the crew chief's head as blood seeped into the Thai soil. "All right everyone, back to work," ordered the line chief. We found out later that the crew chief was married with six kids and had received a Dear John letter from his wife. He had put the flare pistol to his head and pulled the trigger. His war was over.

****

We continued to rebuild our gunship, sweating in the grueling sun handling hot metal day after day. We patched the rest of the holes and had replaced all the major components. Our new wing and engines were painted black to match the rest of the aircraft. It was almost Christmas.

One day, the Bob Hope troupe flew into Ubon and set up stage 100 yards from my aircraft. We enjoyed the show along with almost everyone else on base, with my gunship as a backdrop. It had only been a couple of months since I had left home, but the sight of American girls was astounding! There were no "round eyes" here in remote Thailand and these American gals were captivating to say the least. I had seen Bob Hope in movies and in film clips from all his years of entertaining the troops. It was surreal to see him standing now, just a few feet away, cracking jokes and putting us all at ease. At the end of the show the whole cast came out on stage and sang "Silent Night." Everyone in the crowd that could stand did so, as we all sang along. It sent ripples up and down my spine. Looking around I didn't see a dry set of eyes anywhere. For a fleeting few moments, I felt normal again. It was great! Then, the song was over and so too the feeling.

Christmas came and went. It was just another hot day on the flight line. I received a "care package" from my family back home, which really lifted my spirits. Inside were all my favorite candies, along with some magazines and pictures of family. On the bottom of the box under a bag of homemade cookies, I found a cassette tape. Side one was a recording of current rock songs from a local FM station, including the DJ giving weather reports and concert news. Listening to the tape made me feel almost at home, and it felt good. Side two had the whole family coming on to raise my spirits, offer encouragement or make me laugh. The sound of their voices as they related local happenings was soothing, yet it reminded me of how far away they actually were. I felt the distance was becoming more than geographical.

****

One day, while sitting on the flight line in front of my aircraft, I saw a black U-2 spy plane taxi past the Spectre revetments. His wings had drop-off wheels on each side. Without them his long wings, which were filled with fuel, would drag on the ground. Airmen were walking alongside the wingtips to gauge distance. The pilot had the canopy open. I could see him in his spacesuit as he scanned his gauges and prepared for flight. I wondered where he might be going. It would be Laos or North Vietnam, most likely. His altitude levels were classified, but his wearing of the NASA type spacesuit was a strong indication that it was way up there. He waved his gloved hand and gave me a thumbs up. Minutes later, he disappeared into the high clouds.

Another F-4 crashed and burned on the runway. John and I watched from our perch atop our gunships' new wing.

Days later, Sgt. Rhett and I were standing in the shade under our right wing as John was attempting to relate a funny story to me. He was gesturing wildly to make his point. In his story, he shouted "Hey!" to somebody. Only now, as he shouted, the Spectre line truck was driving past. The driver thought John was shouting to him. The truck driver slammed on his brakes! We could see papers and boxes and people flying forward by the sudden stop. The line truck spun around and raced over to us. We didn't have the heart to tell him that we really didn't need him. So John, sounding urgent, asked for a case of oil. The driver simply handed us the oil and went back on his way. John and I looked at each other and burst out laughing.

****

In early January we had a squadron meeting in the base theater and they tallied up the "kills" by aircraft tail number. Then they showed some of the missions as recorded on the aircraft's BDA recorder. We were shown how once a convoy was spotted along the trail, the gunship would go into his left hand orbit and take out the first and last truck in the convoy. This would trap the remaining trucks and we could kill at leisure. Well, almost. We could see some of the devastating Triple A being fired up at our aircraft as well. The narrator explained to us also that some of the drivers were actually chained to their steering wheels by the North

Vietnamese to prevent them from escaping. They were called "suckers" by the aircrews. In one film we could plainly see one "sucker" hacking away at his wrist with what looked like a knife, to avoid the rounds impacting all around him. A direct hit ended his efforts. Happy New Year!

****

One day I walked into the barracks and found a friend of mine sitting on his bed rolling up a bunch of joints. "Here, want one?" he offered.

"Oh, no thanks," I replied.

"Are you sure?" he said. "It's good stuff!"

A couple other guys wandered in and my friend offered some to them as well. They took his offer. Days later outside our barracks Rhett lit up a joint and passed it over. I took it. Most of us were not heavy drinkers and soon discovered an occasional joint now and then took the edge off.

****

John Forsberg's aircraft No. 572 was the first to get the "big gun." They replaced one of the 40mm cannons with the 105mm Howitzer. It was enormous! The crew came back after a trial run and said every time they fired the big gun, its recoil would knock the gunship clear out of its orbit. The technicians worked to change the way the gun was mounted.

****

One night while taking a break, John Rhett noticed a swarm of ants along the side of our revetment. We happened to have a couple of spray cans of paint with us at the time, so we proceeded to attack the ants. Like miniature gunships firing from above, we covered all the ants with our lethal spray. The next morning as we walked out to our gunship, we could see large patterns of red and blue streaks all over the ground! We hadn't realized in the darkness of the night before, the incredible mess we had created. John and I quickly roughed up the dirt with our boots to cover the evidence of our deeds. The lifers probably would have been concerned more about our waste of government paint than our untidy area. As it was, no one ever saw our little war against the ants. We lost the battle, by the way; the ants were back the next night, some in color.

****

By the middle of January we had Zero Four Four ready to fly. We had worked feverishly to get the airplane back on flying status. Every day we watched as the squadron's other aircraft launched into combat and returned. The gunships paraded past our revetment going to and from the runway, their crews waving to us or offering thumbs up, as they thundered by. Most of them had stopped by one time or another, to watch our progress and cheer us on. We knew that they appreciated our efforts and many shook my hand to that effect. Some pitched in and sweated alongside us as we hoisted an engine or props. We knew they cared about these machines almost as much as we did!

Once in a while after the gunships had launched, a lifer would come around looking for something out of place. My day came when I had positioned two stands on the right side of my revetment. It made sense to me, since it was the right side of my gunship that had been damaged. Right now, all of the work was on this side. This particular lifer thought it would "look better" if I had a stand on both sides of the revetment, but not together. It would look "balanced" this way, he said. I tried to explain that it was more important to me to get my craft air-worthy again than to look balanced. I don't think he appreciated my response. I moved the heavy stand to the other side of the revetment. Once he left, I moved it back. The next day he was in my face again. I thought he had his priorities mixed up and told him so. This "game" went on for a few days before he gave up.

I began to notice everyone's attitude had turned more aggressive with each mission. At our poker games with the gunners, they would describe in lurid detail the carnage of the previous night's missions. They talked of explosions, fireballs and vehicles being obliterated by 40mm shells. They described what 20mm shells do to a body or a group of soldiers. One gunner described how a panicked VC driver jumped from his damaged truck and ran down the dark road. Just then Spectre walked the "twenties" right down his back and beyond with a quick and precise burst of her miniguns. Part of me was glad that at least for the moment, I was not contributing to the carnage.

****

By 1972, virtually all American ground troops had left Vietnam. We couldn't say we were killing the enemy to prevent them from killing our guys because American troops were for the most part, gone. Sure we may have prevented South Vietnamese soldiers from dying, but no one wanted to be the last American to die in Vietnam. We were pulling out! We had all seen or heard about the anti-war protests back in the States. It seemed like we were killing just because we had the technology to do it. And, we were very good at what we did.

Some of the fellows I had known before Spectre were growing more militant. They were caught up in the grand spectacle of war. Some turned to drink as a diversion, others to hard drugs, including heroin. These were guys I'd known back in the World as being straight and narrow. We had to literally dress and pack the bags of one fellow who was so strung out on heroin he couldn't do it himself. We put him on the plane when his time to go home had arrived. I don't know if he made it or not.

My sitting on the sidelines, however, would not last much longer.

****

My aircraft was ready now for flight-testing. We had put everything back together and run tests in the revetment. Now we had to be sure it could fly again. We were scheduled for a daylight local mission "around the flag pole." I rode along. It felt like any other C-130 I had flown in before. That is until the pilot decided to bore-sight the guns. There was a patch of jungle not far from our flight line where the gunships could test the alignment of their guns. Burrrraattt!! I just about jumped out of my seat. I was riding in an empty chair in the booth when the 20mm guns were fired. I wasn't ready for the noise. Burrrraattt!! I came out of the booth and it was louder still. The ramp was up and the door was open. I could see the ground below and behind us. I imagined myself hanging over the edge with Triple-A coming up amid all this noise as our guns fired back. I was glad I didn't pursue the IO position.

We had enough glitches on this maiden flight to ground the aircraft for two more days, during which time I painted our names on the side as crew chiefs. Finally we were put back into the flying rotation, and the real fun began.

"Ready to start No. 3?" came the pilot's voice on the intercom.

"No. 3 is clear," I responded.

"Starting engine No. 3," the pilot said. The rush was indescribable as I stood before my gunship, its new engines roaring to life. I wanted retribution for the damage to my ship. Now, she was ready for the fight. John and I, along with a host of other maintenance crews, had brought Zero Four Four back to life. Now her crewmen were about to risk theirs.

It had been about two months, but we were back in action again. I marshaled my aircraft out of the revetment and to the arming area. Once all four engines were running, I gave the pilot a salute, then offered a quick thumbs up. He returned both and headed out. When the aircraft was airborne, John and I rode back to the snack bar and joined the other crew chiefs.

A few hours later, the gunships started returning. When No. 044 landed, the line chief suggested we park it along the main row of revetments. The spot we took was right next to the crew chiefs' lounge! We performed our post-flight inspection on the aircraft. I knew now to be always on the lookout for *any* battle damage. Sometimes shrapnel from a close air burst would pepper the wings or tail. The aircrew would not necessarily have seen or heard a minor hit over the din of battle. Thankfully, there was no damage on this night, so we refueled, rearmed and called it a day.

****

The flight crew that brought Zero Four Four back so heroically two months before, were assigned the next mission. I joked with the pilot about all my hours of hard work and sweat, putting the gunship back together. As we did a walk around, I asked him to please bring it back in

Jet mechanics graduation day. I'm in the back row (*4th from the right*). The C-130 prop line leads directly to me and John Forsberg is on my right. Sheppard AFB, Texas, 1970.

Airman 1st Class Combs. Dyess AFB, Texas, 1970.

I was assigned to this C-130E (63-7805) as an assistant crew chief and later became primary crew chief on this same aircraft. Dyess AFB, Texas, 1970.

This was John Forsberg's C-130 (63-7816) with the red cross markings for our hostage rescue mission. Look closely at the bottom right to see my C-130 as well as John Rhett's airplane in the distance. Incirlik Air Base, Turkey, September 1970.

My 1960 Corvette with the custom paint by family friend Bob Walters. I proudly displayed this car at the Taylor County Coliseum's first ever custom car show. Abilene, Texas, 1970.

Tom and Mom outside our little garage apartment in Abilene, Texas, 1970. I bought the 1967 Chevrolet wagon from my brother Jack. (He now re-owns and has completely restored this car. One unique aspect of this station wagon was its factory four-speed!)

Me (*left*) and Forsberg. We had just recently been promoted to A1C. Dyess AFB, Texas, 1970.

Globe Bar. Purchased in Italy in 1971 for Mom. I was lucky to have made it home with this treasure as we were pushing equipment out the back of my C-130 over the Atlantic Ocean to lighten the load. I now have this in my home after Mom passed away in 2007.

Prometheus 55-0044, AC-130A gunship. Notice the three red stars above the crew entrance door. Ubon RTAFB, Thailand, 1971.

I tend to a small engine problem on Prometheus. I'm now Spectre Crew Chief Sgt. Combs.

Battle damage on Zero Four Four (044). Number three and four engines prop assemblies blown off. Notice the wrinkle effect on the cowling from the extreme over torque. November 1971.

Zero Four Four battle damage. Mute testimony to the durability of the C-130 airframe and the heroic efforts of the gunship's crewmen.

Sergeant Johnson and I replace the brakes on 044 after the gunship suffered severe battle damage. November 1971.

Tending to the 20mm guns on Prometheus. This photo was taken by Sgt. Rhett just a few weeks before the AC-130 was shot down. February 1972.

Spectre Emblem from the 16th Special Operations Squadron. "If you ain't Spectre…"

Sergeant Rhett (*left*) and I outside the new air-conditioned barracks. We lived on the second floor. Our bunks were on the far left in this photo, next to the foiled windows of the day room. Ubon, RTAFB, 1972.

Bent Nail Qualified patch given to ground crews for battle damage repair to AC-130 gunships, 1972.

Waiting for the return of my gunship from an early morning combat mission. I always removed my ring once the gunship had landed. I had learned my lesson almost the hard way. January 1972.

Sergeant Bob Wollman outside the crew chiefs' barracks. Notice the silhouettes of the three gunships shot down (044, 571, 043) painted on the door.

Spectre 571. This E-model gunship was one of the first to be outfitted with the 105mm howitzer. This was Sgt. Bob Wollman's aircraft. It was shot down just hours after my gunship was lost, March 29, 1972 (Bob Wollman's birthday). The entire crew was rescued in one of the largest SAR missions of the war.

This is a view of Spectre aft, looking forward from the ramp. Twin 40mm guns on the left and the sensor booth to the right. Notice the row of parachutes just beyond the guns.

Ubon, RTAFB Thailand. The 16th SOS revetments are at the top center of photo. Lower left are the revetments for the Wolfpack 433rd and 435th squadrons of F-4s. Our barracks can be seen at the tip of the triangle of buildings, far left side of photo.

This is a reverse view showing the Spectre revetments. Note the parking spot on the right side center of photo. This is the spot we used when repairing the battle damage to 044 as the revetment was closest to all the maintenance buildings.

Sergeant Forsberg, Ubon, 1972. This photo has John on the barracks' second level landing. The base perimeter is seen in the background. Often trip flares would ignite within the trees interrupting our poker games.

Gunship 572. This was Sgt. Forsberg's E-model gunship showing the four-bladed props in the text book "X" position. This was the first AC-130 to receive the 105mm gun. Looking good John!

AC-130A #509. Good aerial view of Sgt. O'Neill's gunship (56-0509). This aircraft took a hit in the belly directly under the booth. Number 509 retired in 1995 and is on display at The Air Commando Heritage Park, Hurlburt Field, Florida. (*Photo courtesy of Gary Van Cott and The Spectre Association*)

Our last day at Ubon. *Front row, left to right*: John Rhett, me, John Forsberg and our squadron commander. Look closely to see that we were all soaking wet from the Songkran Festival activities. Notice the water pistol in Sgt. Rhett's hand, and typical Sgt. Forsberg with his arm around the commander.

An OV-10 Bronco going through an engine run test on the PSP flight line. This material was very slippery when wet from the monsoon rains. Working on these small and light aircraft was quite a departure from that of the larger C-130s.

Official patch of the 23rd Tactical Air Support Squadron, which was part of the 56th Special Operations Wing flying OV-10s in support of air operations throughout S.E. Asia. This patch reportedly had been designed by Walt Disney Studios.

Sergeants Fred Marshall *(left)* and Dan O'Neill standing just outside the door to my room. Both Airmen came with me from Ubon and Spectre. Fred is the person that inspired me to take up martial arts.

"Sparky," an OV-10 crew chief, became a fast friend to all of us transplants from Ubon. Here in our room he enjoys a cigar while playing air drums to the music on our stereo. Sitting on the floor of this room I heard "Stairway To Heaven" by Led Zeppelin for the first time.

Standing outside my room before heading to the flight line. Notice the mustache and hair growing just a bit beyond Air Force regulations. At this point, I just didn't care.

HC-130H sits on the flight line at Hamilton, AFB, California, 1973. It was a pleasure to be working again on my beloved C-130s. The journey was soon to end as I was about to sign out of the USAF.

one piece. Their mission was relatively uneventful except they had received a SAM warning from the RHAW gear. A SAM was a surface-to-air missile about the size of a telephone pole. Intelligence said there were no SAMs in the Steel Tiger area. They were wrong.

A few nights later, we were in the crew chiefs' lounge when the line truck screeched to a stop outside the door. A sergeant stuck his head in and said, "Five-oh-nine?" "Here," came the sleepy reply from its crew chief. Sergeant O'Neill emerged from the corner of the small room into the light. He looked pissed off to be disturbed from his catnap. Before he could ask any questions, the sergeant waved his arms frantically. I knew what was coming next. "Come with me," he said, "your plane has been hit. It's coming back now."

A number of us followed Dan O'Neill into the waiting van and out to the recovery area. As we rode in complete silence to recovery, I could feel the apprehension Dan was experiencing. Nothing I could say would comfort him. He just stared out the side window of the truck.

Dan was a dark-haired young sergeant from back East somewhere. He had that East Coast accent and temperament to go with it. He was a no nonsense kind of guy. That night he was a guy about to get some very bad news. Arriving in the recovery area just off the main runway the line chief pulled over and turned off the engine. The long silence was deafening. Soon the fire trucks moved into their positions nearby and we all waited. In less than half an hour, we could see the AC-130 on final approach. As it touched down and rolled closer, the "A" model gunship appeared to be perfectly normal. As it moved off the runway onto the apron, a few of us ran over to it. I still could not see any battle damage. The pilot shut down engines and we moved under the wing tips to the back of the aircraft.

"Watch out, make way, make way. Give us some room here."

It was one of the navigators from the booth speaking frantically. They were carrying a crewmember to the ramp. An ambulance pulled alongside and a stretcher appeared. As the crew came off, we jumped on the ramp. I still didn't see any damage.

We entered the booth. Wow! The aircraft took a hit right in the belly.

The explosion tore a hole five feet in diameter right under the IR's chair. The chair was raised up at an odd angle, and twisted metal was everywhere. The whole booth had been torn from its mounts. The Black Crow operator had been hit by shrapnel and cut up pretty bad, but it was the IR that took the brunt of the hit. Tucked in the far left corner of the booth under the instrument panel and amid all the blood was a boot. I negotiated around the gaping hole and reached down to pick it up. It felt heavy. As I turned and handed it to the medic standing in the doorway, I noticed the boot appeared to have part of a foot still in it. Oh shit!

Moving slowly to avoid the jagged edges, I looked down through the hole and saw the yellow line painted on the ground beneath us. Again, we were told not to touch anything until the investigators looked it over. I talked about the mission with the rear scanner as he stood holding his hands clasped together on his head. He looked weary. The scanner said it came out of nowhere, like a tracer-less round. "No warning at all," he said. "Scared the shit out of me." The four navigators in the booth were all hurt. The two navigators seated in back were saved by the consoles in front of them, but the explosion and concussion was enough to burst an eardrum or two. One of the gunners told me that for the entire flight back to Ubon, the BC operator had to hold onto the IR to keep him from falling out through the black hole in the floor!

We helped Sgt. O'Neill tow his aircraft to one of the revetments close to maintenance. Now it was his turn. (This same aircraft later saw action in the Mayaguez incident in May 1975 as well as Panama and Iraq much later. Today, this aircraft sits proudly on permanent display at Hurlburt Field, Florida, in full Vietnam era colors.)

****

One evening while refueling my gunship, I was introduced to Sgt. Mills. The young three-striper was a friend of one of our crew chiefs. He was recently transferred to Ubon from Phu Cat in South Vietnam. Mills was a crew chief on F-4 Phantoms. We gave him a tour of our gunship the following afternoon, leaving him impressed. Not wanting to be outdone, he invited us to his new squadron for a closer look at the

Phantoms. Just a few days later when our aircraft was on a mission, Sgt. Rhett and I ventured over to see him.

Our specialty ratings were the same (Spec code: 43151F). We were, after all, jet mechanics and this was clearly a jet. Almost immediately we discovered they were overwhelmed and undermanned. We were put to work. A number of systems are similar, and I had no trouble working off the checklist. We ended up staying about three or four hours and helped launch the Phantoms. They were heading to North Vietnam to take out a number of bridges. That year, they had new weapons called smart bombs. Some were laser guided. Others had a TV camera in the nose of the bomb and could be directed by the weapon system officer (WSO) in the rear cockpit.

When the pilots came out to do their preflight walk-around, they noted our Spectre hats and had good things to say about the AC-130s.

The Wolf Pack maintenance chief thanked us for assisting, and as we were leaving to head back to our revetments, invited us to their next squadron picnic. We accepted.

At the Wolf Pack picnic a few days later, I munched on barbecued steak and drank cold beer. Our affiliation with Spectre provided us with a warm reception. The crowd was a wide compliment of colorful patches on flight suits. There were AC-130 crews and crews representing F-4s, OV-10s, EC-47s and a few helicopter folks. The EC-47 was the old venerable Gooney bird and was used to spy on the enemy's radio communications. I noticed the "Barons," which was their call-sign, kept a little to themselves and didn't talk about their mission. The Phantom pilots however were just the opposite. They were loud and boastful. Captains Steve Richie and Chuck DeBellevue were visiting that day and talked about F-4 escort missions with our AC-130s. Captain Richie preferred to hunt MIGs. (Later that year, he would become the first USAF Ace of the war with five MIG kills. Captain DeBellevue would become the leading ace of the war with six kills!) I discovered after talking with various pilots at the picnic, that a special group of them were called the Night Owls. These were the pilots and aircraft used for the escort missions with Spectre. They were an impressive group.

****

Things were heating up in the Steel Tiger area and our gunships were flying now every night. Smitty was the IO on tonight's mission. He jokingly gave me the finger from the back of the gunship, as they lifted off the runway. He was becoming a good friend. Hours later when they returned though, he was in a much different mood. "Man we killed a bunch of trucks out there tonight," he told me as we sat down.

The crew bus had not arrived yet, so Smitty had just dropped his gear and himself on the ground in exhaustion. While we waited, he began to tell me about the mission. He said they had started a number of secondary fires, but he had seen more Triple-A tonight than ever before. "Sometimes that stuff arcing up actually looks beautiful, but not tonight," he said, "not tonight."

Smitty shook his head back and forth sweat still pouring off his face. "It was unreal man, I'm tellin' ya, and I've never seen anything like it. The AC was cool though, I'd call break and we'd roll out and then he would put us right back into orbit, firing practically the whole time!" The AC that Smitty was referring to was the aircraft commander.

The blue Air Force bus rolled to a stop out front and the rest of the crew slowly walked over and began to board. Smitty got to his feet and I followed him to the front of my aircraft. "Major Ramsower is not afraid of any of that shit Charlie throws up at us. If he had his way, we'd attack the guns instead of the trucks." Smitty walked away mumbling, helmet in his hand. "Unreal man…just unreal."

Some days later while walking through preflight together, the flight engineer brought up the story of the second gunship lost to ground-fire. It was No. 625, shot down over the Ho Chi Minh Trail in April 1970 by Triple-A. It had been dueling with the guns on the ground. "Only one crewman was rescued, while the rest are MIA. No one knows whether they are dead or alive," he said flatly. "Thirty-seven millimeter hit in the aft fuselage section."

The next time I encountered this same engineer, he told me of another Spectre legend. About a year before 625 was lost, Spectre made history with its first ever air- to-air kill. Opening his arms wide and gesturing to my aircraft, he said, "This gunship, *Prometheus*, shot down an enemy helicopter in flight. They encountered it below them as they were returning to base after a mission over the Trail." I pointed to the three red stars above the crew entrance opening. "Yeah. That was the first star," he said, "I don't know the full story of the other two."

Before I had a chance to relate the similar story of the third star, he was called over by the aircraft commander. A short time later as the engineer was jumping onboard my gunship, I asked how he knew of such things, he stated simply, "I was here in ' 69."

No one talked about it, but everyone wondered if there would be a third gunship shot down and which airplane would it be?

****

Toward the end of January we launched our aircraft as always, but this time it returned about two hours later. They had taken an air burst directly in front of the aircraft and the shrapnel destroyed one of the windshields. The pilot told me it scared the living hell out of him! I toiled in the hot sun the entire next day trying to get the damaged window out and a new one installed. It was probably the original glass from when the aircraft rolled off the assembly line back in 1955!

That night after working on our aircraft, a few of us stopped at the post office to pick up our mail. We headed over to one of the sandbagged bunkers that were scattered around the base. Once inside, I started to read my letter from home by the flickering flame of my lighter. My Aunt Clara had died. Someone passed around a joint. No one noticed the tears running down my cheeks in the darkness.

****

Life in the new barracks was comfortable. We lived in a new two-story building. Each floor had two open bays with an enclosed shower space and latrine in the center. We created small living spaces by moving our lockers around. John Rhett and I used an old wood ammo box to house our expanding stereos. It was a nice diversion in planning our stereo or camera purchases. We would pour over the literature of each brand, comparing features and quality. For me, it was a reminder that there was a life beyond all this. Our barracks were right next to the gunners' and scanners' barracks, so we didn't have far to go to find a poker game. Time off (what little we had), was usually filled with music and cards.

Among some of the other crew chiefs in our barracks, John and I discovered Bob Wollman. Bob was from Seattle as well and was fortunate to crew a newer "E" model, gunship No.571. We spent hours telling stories of home, sharing memories of a familiar area. Sergeant Wollman was a tall man, solidly built. He and some others in fact were now studying karate. The base had a small study hall for that purpose. I had seen them on occasion outside practicing in the hot sun. That's not for me I thought. I felt safer having Sgt. Wollman around sometimes though, especially when we ventured off base.

Trip flares were going off more frequently now, and we continued taking them for granted. Our barracks were on the outer perimeter of the base and at the opposite end from the flight line. We would gather on our second floor balcony and watch the flares trickle down in their little parachutes. We'd watch the area, waiting for something or someone to come into view. Very quickly, the Air Police in the armored personnel carriers (APCs) would pull up and they would all go out to investigate. Usually it was just a water buffalo or a snake, but not always.

Because our barracks were so distant from the flight line, a number of us decided to buy bicycles as a more efficient mode of travel. John Rhett and I split the cost to buy a used one. It belonged to a Spectre gunner who was ending his tour and rotating home. We became like kids again. Sometimes we careened around the base on our single speed old style bikes for hours. For me, it was an escape to a time when life was easier. We were also safe on the bikes, as it would be harder for the snakes to bite our feet or ankles.

John and I could ride double on our bike, with me sitting on the handlebars and John pedaling. If I leaned in one direction, it was hard for John to steer in another, so I controlled our directions and John controlled the speed and brakes. That was the idea anyway. We had our share of crashes and splashes. We scraped a few staff cars along the road and left more than a few Airmen behind us with raised fists. Sorry guys. After a while though, we were smooth and capable.

From our barracks, we traveled partly along a dirt trail. It was over a large grassy field on our way to the flight line. In recent months, cobras or deadly kraits had been found and killed in that same field. I was glad to be up on a bike and zooming by instead of on foot. More than once the line truck would pull up to the revetment late some afternoon to proudly show us their "kill." The snakes were usually large, filling a good portion of the pickup bed.

Once, during a post-flight inspection of Zero Four Four, I noticed a cassette in the tape recorder on the navigator's table. I pushed the rewind button and put on a headphone nearby. Easing myself into the navigator's chair I took a deep breath and pushed the play button. The tape started with a bang! I sat transfixed listening to the audio of the last mission. It was amazing to sit in the very cockpit listening to events that happened only an hour before. As the tape played on I could imagine the bright flashes of flares and anti-aircraft artillery bursting outside these windows as the aircrew battled the NVA over the Trail. I lost count of how many times the scanners called out Triple-A. I shut off the machine and sat for a few moments. I wish that I could describe the feeling, but I can't. Only another crew chief perhaps, who has sent his steed into battle and back again, could know. The carnage that transpired and was captured on tape was still resonating through this enormous machine...my machine. The flight crew was long gone by now, so I grabbed the tape and told Sgt. Rhett what I had. We agreed this discovery was probably a "once-in-a-lifetime" thing, so I rode my bike back to the barracks and copied the tape to my cassette. I pedaled back to the flight line and placed the tape back in the recorder on the NAV's table.

Early the next morning, we listened to the entire tape. It was eerie. I recognized the voices and could see their faces in my mind. I felt like I was there with them. This was after all, my aircraft. I only loaned it to these guys each night for them to use.

The tape contained not only the voices within the gunship, but also that of the F-4 escorts and other aircraft flying over Laos that night. The navigator must have just popped the tape into his machine when things got interesting.

"Hey! Let's move off of this…"

"Hey, I got a light that came off at 4 o'clock under the clouds…and it's still lit!"

"Roger, I got it! "

"Ok, no sweat, let's take it easy."

"How's it lookin'?"

"The flares are below us."

"There's Triple-A at 3 o'clock!"

"No sweat."

"Roll out one two zero pilot."

"Seven rounds of thirty- seven…"

"Rog, one two zero."

"They're harassing us."

"Nav…IR…note for that target, I counted seven hot spots on the road."

"Rog…"

"Harass? Scared the shit out of me!"

"That's affirm, baby!"

"I think that must be a first."

"I'd never seen it before."

"What'd we get?"

"Seven flares above the aircraft…"

"Let's check and see if there's somebody above us!"

"Not like these…these are artillery flares…I saw `em coming up!"

"These came from the ground goddamn it!"

"Okay…"

"They went right over the wing!"

"Should I log seven flares accurate?"

"They were damn close to us."

"Right up the tail!"

"Okay…ah…one two zero…let's go somewhere…"

"Triple-A!! Break left…left!!"

"Hold whatcha got pilot…HOLD whatcha got!!"

"Okay."

"I got it."

"Twelve rounds...thirty-seven..."

"That's no sweat...take it easy right scanner."

"It looked like they were hookin' right into us from here, sir."

"There's three fires on the ground where we were...pilot."

"Yeah..."

"Right at 9 o'clock."

"Yeah...they got a sucker trapped in there..." (Click...click...)

"For you students...this is NOT a standard mission!"

"Roger that!"

"There's Triple-A at 2 o'clock!"

"Triple-A at 3 o'clock! No threat."

"Eleven rounds..."

"Take it IR."

"IR's got another target...take IR guidance."

"IR's in."

"Triple-A ...6 o'clock...fifty-seven...two rounds..."

"And you're cleared to fire Pilot...in this area."

"Four rounds of fifty-seven...no threat!"

"Six rounds of fifty-seven...no threat!"

"Triple-A ...9 o'clock...no threat!" "Five rounds...thirty-seven..."

"Triple-A ...12 o'clock!"

"COMING UP THE NOSE!!"

"I got it ahh...just hold whatcha got..."

"No threat!"

"Seven rounds...fifty-seven."

"'Tis an interesting night!"

"Triple-A...4 o'clock...no threat!"

"Six rounds of fifty-seven..."

"Triple-A underneath! No threat...ten rounds...fifty-seven."

"This is Moonbeam on Guard with a warning to all aircraft. Avoid X-ray Delta three- zero-zero...three-zero-zero on the two-six-five degree radial... Fifty-seven nautical miles...channel one-oh-three Tacan...avoid from now until twelve-fifty Zulu... this is Moonbeam on Guard...out!"

"Pilot...Nav...pull up the flaps and put the coals to it!"

"Okay, where we going?"

"We're going out from under an Arc-light!"

"Okay, I got the aircraft."

"Triple-A underneath!…No threat…eight rounds of fifty-seven!"

"I had an air-burst at 11 o'clock…"

"Well…we'll enjoy an Arc-light yet, Gair."

"Yeah."

"Hey, Gair?"

"Yeah…"

"How's your gray hair?"

"Ah…yeah, I'm growin' gray hair now I'll tell ya'…"

"Triple-A underneath! No threat…still comin' up! It's fifty-seven, six rounds!

"It 'tis nice to know they're taking a interest."

"TRIP…!"

"Come on scanner!"

"No threat!"

"Say what?"

"Don't be afraid to call them my boy…"

"How many rounds, Gair?"

"Looked like twenty." (Click…click...)

"I'm just trying to give you a chance to call it …"

"And now make sure you call the position too."

"Triple-A 9 o'clock…"

"Roger…Engineer's got it…no sweat."

"Nine rounds…thirty-seven!"

"Triple-A 5 o'clock!"

"Triple-A 6 o'clock!"

"Roger…no threat. Thirty rounds, thirty-seven…they got guns all along that river we just crossed over."

"Triple-A ACCURATE!"

"Break right… RIGHT!

"ROLL OUT!"

"Okay…roll back!"

"Four rounds...fifty-seven..."
"Arc-lights at 3 o'clock!"
"Triple-A 6 o'clock...no threat. Twelve rounds, fifty-seven!"
"Roger, copy."
"Triple-A 6 o'clock! No threat...ten rounds...thirty-seven."
"IR's got another possible target."
"There's Bandits heading'this way...they're up by Squid now..."
"Triple-A 6 o'clock No threat! Ten rounds thirty-seven."
"Okay, ah...one forward... Give me another good burst...NOW!"
"DIRECT HIT! Large explosion..."
"Yeah...I got visual..."
"Large explosion...medium fire!"
"Roger!"

****

Things were obviously heating up for our aircrews, as increasing numbers of Triple-A were being fired at them. Some of the guys talking around our poker table one night explained that Charlie was bringing in more guns to defend his trail network and the NVA were increasing their traffic down the Trail. Intelligence suspected something big was brewing.

The AC-130s increased their nightly truck kills. Spectre had been, by now, credited with close to ten-thousand truck kills! Our Special Ops squadron operated 14 Spectre AC-130s only. You can do the math.

It wasn't only trucks, of course. Spectre had knocked out all types of vehicles from tanks to bicycles. Even elephants, riverboats and sampans were targets. Their numbers were in the hundreds by now this season alone. The beer was flowing. The human costs, of course were much higher.

Sometimes the Vietcong were fanatical in their charge of a firebase. Spectre would roll into orbit around the base and selectively annihilate the enemy with the 20mm guns. The aircrews were usually quiet and sullen after those missions. One evening while the crew milled around after one such mission, one of the scanners approached me and simply announced, "Cordwood." Shaking his head he continued in a soft voice,

"We rolled into orbit and made a quick pass over the target. There were hundreds of them pouring into the center. With each pass we stopped the next wave right as they were crawling over their dead. Even from altitude we could see how high the stacks of bodies were getting. It was suicidal for them but they just kept coming."

The enemy was, in fact, paying dearly. The squadron body count since November was so high as to be obscene. I was beginning to feel the madness! I was being immersed in all this death. I swear, sometimes I could smell it on the gunship after a mission.

Isn't all this wrong? Why is everyone shooting and dying? What about "Thou shall not kill"? I was in a moral dilemma. I was proud of being a sergeant in the Air Force and an accomplished crew chief. I took great pride in my aircraft. I had come a long way. But all this death seemed so extreme. Each night I was unleashing a dark predator that destroyed anything or anyone in its path. I tried to distance myself from the process. The attitude of the air and ground crews was businesslike. Everyone was just doing his own individual job. We all had our positions and responsibilities. Still, the duties and decisions I made today played a part in how many would die tonight. We justified it by saying we were killing communists.

I tried to focus on preparations for my R&R. I was to meet Denise and Tracy in Hawaii in a few months and that gave me something to look forward to. I worried about what I was becoming and I felt like I would be a stranger to my family.

Some of the other crew chiefs had moved off base into shacks downtown. They had "tee-locks" or live-in girlfriends. These "tee-locks" would usually string a few GIs along at the same time. Each GI thinking his girl was with him and only him. They sure took a lot of trips away to visit "Mom," and of course needed money to help the "family." I saw through it right away and had no desire to be fleeced by a Thai con artist. If we needed female companionship, there were always the bathhouses. We were working six days a week and usually fourteen hours a day. We didn't have much time to explore the neighborhood.

We did check out the bars one night, to listen to some of the local bands. A popular song at the time was "Joy To The World" by Three Dog Night. The song's opening line was "Jeremiah was a bullfrog... he was a good friend of mine." As we walked into one bar, the Thai lead singer belted out, "Jezzamia was a boo-fog, he was a goo fen of my." We just looked at each other and laughed. Most of the bands actually sounded pretty good, I'll give them that. But the language did prove to be a musical barrier.

One fellow crew chief brought his tee-lock to the NCO club one night. While he was getting us another round of beers, I tried out my Thai language skills on his girl. I was trying to ask her if she had ever smoked a joint. I got a very surprised look from her as I asked her in her native tongue. A couple of guys at the table almost fell over laughing. I wasn't sure what they found so funny. When her boyfriend came back with the drinks, she whispered something in his ear and he let out a howl. It seems I asked her unknowingly to perform oral sex on me. We all enjoyed a laugh over that for some time.

****

There was another probe at the perimeter and this time we watched the security police haul away a man who was crawling under the wire. We never did hear what he was up to. He was barefoot and wearing black. That was enough for me.

****

A small group of us took the Baht bus to downtown Ubon a few miles away. It was a harrowing experience. The bus was almost miniature in size and we were cramped to begin with, but then they overloaded the vehicle. During the ride we had people actually hanging on outside the bus as well. The driver would pass on hills and around curves and more than once knocked someone off their bicycle as we roared past.

A large part of downtown Ubon had been destroyed by fire months before and was very depressing. Much of the city was dirty and smelled horrible. We walked to the bridge crossing the Mun River (pronounced *moon* river). On the other side was a U.S. Army base of some sort. The river was brown and running slowly. Someone in our group started singing, "Moon river, wider than a mile, I've come to you in style...." All of us groaned in unison. We checked out the hotels and restaurants and a theatre by the large traffic circle. Large posters hung from the nearby buildings with Thai lettering showing titles and actors in numerous movies now showing. Of course not knowing the language we had no idea what the movies were about other than by the "action" photos on the posters. "Hey, we should check out a Thai movie," John Rhett whispered as we walked by the theatre door. "Yeah," I muttered without giving it much thought. I was mesmerized by the whole scene of the city and its people going about their daily lives.

One of the guys we were with bought a pack of "ready rolls" from a taxi driver. These were marijuana cigarettes pre-rolled and packaged, including cellophane on the box. Four of us split two cigarettes. The others quickly started making comments about how good the effects were. I was feeling nothing out of the ordinary. On my next inhale I held my breath. The other guys, including John Rhett, were talking up a storm about the wild perceptions flooding their minds. Still, I was feeling normal. I thought they were joking about what they were experiencing. *Maybe these were just regular Thai cigarettes and these guys are messin' with me,* I thought as we continued to walk on into the night. We had by now moved away from all remnants of town. It was completely dark, like the night in Germany. I realized, as we glided through the black night, that I was seeing as if it were a hazy day. All things around me carried a strange glow. This glow allowed me to "see" in the dark. When I realized what I was feeling and seeing, it overwhelmed me! Now my senses were discovering things around me in a way I had never before observed. I lost all track of time and floated along in the light. The light only I had found in the darkness. I kept waiting for someone in black pajamas to jump out from the side of the road. I needed the comfort of familiar surroundings and suggested it to the group.

We came across a little village. Two of us wandered into a tailor's shop. Everything was in miniature. I remember ducking just to get in the door. I was mesmerized by the variety of all the different fabrics. With my "glowing" vision, all this was reverberating with light. One of the guys grabbed me, and we headed back outside. Somehow we managed to buy a Coke at a street-side café. From my perspective the people around us glowed and sparkled. I was aware of my voice talking, but I didn't know it was me. This was too much. We went to a friend's hooch nearby. It helped to sit down and not move. I listened to music and continued to ride this wave of uncertainty. My friend offered his tee-lock to me for comfort, but I didn't want to move. Sometime later, we ventured outside again. We caught an old run-down bus and headed back to the airbase. It had been hours since I had smoked, but still its effects were enveloping me. Later I was told these joints were laced with opium. That was a very scary night and I vowed never to touch those again.

Back on the flight line we continued to put in long hours and toiled under the hot tropical sun. The older "A" model C-130s required more attention that the newer "E" models. I envied my buddies who were assigned to the newer aircraft. The pressure was immense to keep our aircraft flying.

As I rode my bicycle back to the barracks early one morning, I noticed security police all around our barracks. They had sealed off one entire section of the building. My first thought was, "Oh no, someone is getting busted." I showed my ID to the policeman in front of the door. He allowed me in but told me to stay out of the other end of the building. A short time later, I ventured over to get a peek. On our second floor, on the opposite side, another airman tried to take his own life. There was blood all over his locker and across the floor. Apparently, quite distraught, the young sergeant stabbed himself multiple times with a butter knife. He lived through his ordeal, but we never saw him again.

****

One night in early February, we had just reached our seats in the base theater when the picture went blank, and the house lights came on. My first thought was another broken film, which was rather common, but soon we heard the sirens. The loudspeaker in the theater came on and we were told to report to our duty stations, "Condition Red." The base was under attack! Oh shit! I thought, as we ran outside through the side exit and down to the Spectre maintenance shack. Rumors about what was happening ranged from "this is a test" to "this is an all out assault." We soon discovered that it was not a test. Gunfire erupted from the flight line perimeter. I had no idea whether it was ours or "theirs."

It was suggested we get to our aircraft and be prepared to get them moved. An enemy sapper hopes to gain access to as many airplanes as possible. Our revetments would minimize collateral damage if one gunship is targeted, but a moving target is harder to hit. Not to mention an airborne and orbiting Spectre is perfect for the job of perimeter defense and base security.

About twenty crew chiefs stood under the Spectre sign as the Maintenance Chief gathered news from his walkie-talkie. "Aircrews are on their way...but you better get to your gunships pronto," the chief bellowed, "Pull covers, streamers, chocks and start 'em up...!" I ran out to my gunship. John Rhett was already there. Together we removed all ground equipment and B-1 stands. We pulled streamers and intake covers at a gallop. Almost like it was planned, John and I pulled chalks simultaneously from both sides of the airplane. I followed Rhett as he jumped up on the ramp after tossing the big yellow chalks inside. From memory, we made our way in the dark to the flight deck. Right away John slid into the flight engineer's seat and switched on power. The overhead lights came on suddenly and I remember feeling exposed. John switched the flight deck lighting to red as I moved past him and sat in the pilot's seat. Both of us grabbed some headphones and plugged in. We began engine startup procedures. The aircrews had not shown up yet, but we were ready if need be. As I sat in the pilot's seat, John was almost beside me leaning over from the engineer's chair. He was scanning the overhead panel. We used the check list to start engines No. 2 and No. 3. In just a short amount of time we had accomplished a striking number of tasks with immediacy. The feeling was indescribable. What an amazing and swift chain of events that brought me from sitting in a theatre chair to sitting in the pilot's seat of my gunship with engines roaring outside.

I looked at John as he gazed at the overhead panel. We figured the tower could give us some good information so I switched on the radios. There was chatter and a few raised voices back and forth. We listened intently, trying to figure out what to do next. I was ready to taxi out at a moment's notice or any sign of trouble outside. The notice came but it was to shut down engines. We breathed a collective sigh of relief. I could taxi the aircraft but not fly it. Together we shut down the engines using the checklist. John just looked at me, and we both started to laugh. What a rush!

About an hour later, a pickup truck slowly made the rounds throughout the Spectre revetments. In the back of the truck was the source of all the excitement. Dressed in black shorts, with a knapsack full of explosives, was the dead sapper. There had been others the Air Police said, but they were caught and being held for interrogation. "This one tried to avoid capture," he said as he poked at the body. With that, he jumped back into his truck and took his show on the road. I wasn't in the mood to watch a movie after that.

The following day we had a meeting in the maintenance building. Our squadron commander was present. In essence, he said those of us who had aircraft in the revetments last night, and brought to combat readiness, had acted professionally. He was proud of us. We all looked at each other and the room erupted into applause. It felt good...real good. The base increased its security after that.

About a week after the sapper attack, we were told that because the war was winding down (it was?), once we had been in-country for six months we could apply for an early out. That would mean I could rotate back to the World by the middle of April. I brought this up in my letters home to Denise. We decided that R&R in Hawaii was no longer necessary, as I could be home for good in a couple of months. It sounded too good to be true (it was). I signed up for early release and went back to work.

I became friendly with a number of aircrews, and by now had my favorites. Some I dreaded flying my airplane, as they would return with page after page of write-ups, usually chicken-shit stuff that had no bearing on the mission or the aircraft's performance. Once written up, however, they had to be attended to. Other crews were more realistic and only pointed out items crucial to the performance of the aircraft. They knew we put in long hard hours to keep 'em flying and didn't want to add to the burden. Major Ramsower was this way and usually complimented me on having a well-maintained machine.

****

Another Phantom came limping back from a mission and crashed trying to land. The jet was consumed by fire and neither pilot nor back-seater got out. Some rescue people tried to get to them but were driven back by the flames. The flag at Wing Headquarters would be lowered to half-mast for a few days, then raised again. Sometimes with so many pilots being lost, it wasn't raised for weeks at a time.

****

I continued to have my meals, whenever possible, in the NCO club. The base had a chow hall but it was not air-conditioned. It cost more to eat at the NCO club, but the cool air was worth the extra amount. I met Smitty there one day and while I ate my lunch, he drank his. I knew what he and the others faced each night. I certainly would do the same. Some preferred to drink, while others turned to a joint or two. "American Pie," by Don McLean was playing again on the juke-box: "...Drove my Chevy to the levee but the levee was dry / Them good old boys were drinkin' whiskey and rye / Singin' this'll be the day that I die / This'll be the day that I die..."

Sometimes, nothing seemed real anymore. For some that song proved to be all too real. The ones I knew took a fatalistic approach. "If I die, I die."

****

Early one morning the first week of March, John Forsberg got the call we all regretted. "Sergeant Forsberg aren't you tail number 572?" asked the silhouette in the doorway. Before John could stand up the voice added, "Your aircraft has taken a hit and is on the way back. Everyone is okay, and the damage is not critical." The line chief let the door close behind him as he added, "Be ready."

We all started asking questions at the same time. The chief had no answers. A few of the guys left the crew chief's lounge to follow Sgt. Forsberg to the line truck. We piled in the back of the blue pickup and began the long drive to the recovery area. Roughly an hour later, John's gunship landed and taxied to the revetments. The crew emerged as the props slowed to a stop. The damage, caused by a 57mm hit, was in the right wing flap area.

Discussions were held with the idea of moving the big gun to another aircraft. However, the speedy arrival of another 105mm gun from the States eliminated that idea. John was busy for the next few weeks handling the repairs. The newly arrived 105mm gun was installed into another "E"-model gunship, tail number 571. That was Bob Wollman's bird.

When the aircrews of Spectre suited up for a mission it was all business. The crews that I became associated with were nothing short of professional. Those flying my gunship were, in my opinion, the best and the bravest. In spite of heavy Triple-A, more and more battle damage, these aircrew continued to fly and fight. They had guts…pure and simple.

On occasion, when crews or crewmembers had completed their tour they were doused in water to celebrate. It was always fun to watch, and we were all a bit envious of those who were about to rotate home. Captain Halpin was a TV navigator in the booth having just completed his last mission before rotating home. The captain was now hiding inside the booth as his crew-mates gathered nearby. Water had splashed against the booth as he initially started to leave. Halpin was well aware that the crew had been hiding in anticipation of his soaking. After slipping and sliding his way from nose to tail on the wet floor, the captain was boxed in. He finally emerged at the rear of the aircraft and was lifted in the air and carried to the left wingtip where he was hosed down. The crews were like little kids sometimes as they chased each other in and around the gunship splashing everyone gleefully. We usually got some of the water splashed on us, as well, but in this heat it was refreshing. The crews sure as hell deserved the fun and release, but as crew chiefs we had to clean up the mess inside the airplane.

****

One afternoon, Smitty and I talked about some recent missions over the Trail. He offered to get me assigned to an upcoming flight if I wanted. I could go as a "student" scanner, maybe kick out a few flares. I told him I'd think about it. He told me about his R&R plans coming up in April. Smitty, like me, would not have his R&R, but for an entirely different reason.

NINE

Missing In Action

ONE BY ONE THE CREW EMERGED FROM THE CREW BUS. Loaded down with their combat helmets and equipment they walked slowly to the rear of my airplane and started to climb aboard. Smitty was real gunner, and he slapped me on the back as he strolled by. I turned quickly to push him back on his shoulder, moving just in time to avoid being hit by his swinging helmet. We were playing a strange version of tag it seemed. Playfully, I stuck out my middle finger. He smiled as he threw his gear onboard and jumped inside. I was surprised to see Capt. Halpin suited up and standing with the crew.

Apparently there was a mix-up in the schedule and the crew was in need of a TV, so Halpin just volunteered...even though his tour was over. These guys loved their job and they really loved each other. Captain Halpin should have been sitting in the O Club sipping a beer before taking his Freedom Bird home, but instead he volunteered for a combat mission. Watching the young captain jump on the ramp grabbing his gear, I remember wondering—are we going to go through the whole water ritual again when they come back?

"Chief, we're ready to start No. 3." The voice was crisp and clear in my headset. I was now standing in front of my aircraft just off the nose, as John Rhett pulled a fire bottle alongside.

"No. 3 is clear," I replied.

"Starting No. 3," said Maj. Ramsower.

As we went through our engine startup, I felt that I had definitely drawn a good crew tonight. The pilot and I had done our preflight walk-around and as usual, he was pleased with how the aircraft looked.

With two engines running, we marshaled him out of the revetment. John and I jumped into the back of the line truck, and we followed Zero Four Four down to the arming area. I could feel the heat from my gunship's two running engines as we followed behind in its wake. Once in the arming area, I dismounted the truck on a run. As I moved toward the left front of the aircraft, I could see the TV camera following me. The guys in the booth have found their first target. I gave the camera lens the thumbs up as I passed by. John stood by with the fire bottle, ready for anything. John and I usually rotated the duties. Sometimes I would stand by with the fire bottle while John did engine start.

Now plugged back on interphone, I cleared the pilot to start the remaining two engines. John followed me closely with the extinguisher. With all this jet fuel and ammunition on board, the last thing we wanted is a fire of any kind. Quick reflexes would save lives and equipment. We had to be ready for anything.

"Spectre one-three, is ready for takeoff, Chief," said the major.

"Roger," I replied. "Good luck and good hunting."

Moving swiftly, I unplugged myself from the aircraft, coiled up my interphone cord and moved out in front of my AC-130. With the headphones still on my head to dampen the roar of the engines, I gave the pilot a crisp salute and thumbs up. He nodded his helmet, gave me the thumbs up and saluted back as he began moving out to the runway. As the gunship moved past me, with its left wing tip actually passing over my head, hot air from her turbines enveloped me. I leaned into the blast of hot exhaust holding on to my hat. I looked away for a moment to avoid the sting of tiny particles to my face. When I turned around again, I could see the gunners in the back adjusting equipment and moving around. I noticed Smitty standing by the 40mm guns and gave him the peace sign. He flipped me the bird along with a smile. Seconds later, my gunship roared down the runway lifting into the twilight sky. I watched for a moment as it made a gentle left turn, disappearing into the mist. The low rumble of her turboprop engines were now obliterated by the roar of two F-4s streaking over our heads in full afterburner.

I never saw Smitty, my gunship…or the others again.

We rode back to the snack bar and joined the other crew chiefs. They also had just launched their gunships. More ground crews gathered in the twilight as the remaining Spectres were sent into battle.

We often boasted among ourselves, as to which of us owned the best gunship. Our competition was friendly and only strengthened our pride in our individual aircraft. We were part of an elite group and we knew it. Of course mine was without a doubt the best gunship in the squadron.

A few hours later, I was on the flight line under the lights of the revetment, helping another crew chief work on his airplane. Suddenly, the line truck pulled up to the ramp with a screeching of tires. The line chief saw me and waved me over to the truck.

"Your aircraft is down," he said.

"You mean it's been hit again?" I asked.

"It's worse than that," he said, "come with me."

I jumped down off the ramp of the other gunship and came around to the passenger side of the truck and slid inside.

"Zero Four Four was struck by two SAM missiles," he said. "Your aircraft has crashed! Search and Rescue are moving to the scene right now. The F-4 escort pilots saw it happen. They heard a few emergency beepers and are standing by."

By this time, we had found John Rhett in another revetment and were now headed to Squadron Operations where we could monitor the search and rescue. I was numb. I could not believe this was happening.

In Squadron Operations, they were gathered around the radios listening to the conversation between the fighters and the rescue helicopters. I stood there in a daze listening to the radio chatter. The F-4s, now running low on fuel, would return to Ubon. Two others had been dispatched to replace them. There was still no word on survivors. Numerous fires were on the ground, but no signs of life. Then, the word came down that a number of beepers were heard again. Was it our guys? Or were the North Vietnamese trying to lure our rescue crews into an ambush? I was stunned!

We left the Squadron Operations Center and walked to the F-4 revetments to meet up with the pilots who had seen it happen. Our squadron's commander was already there.

According to the pilots, the AC-130 was in a valley a few miles west of Tchepone, Laos. The gunship was working over targets in the area. Visibility was about four miles with scattered clouds at 6,000 feet. The aircraft was illuminated by the full moon to the west, a gunner's moon. Triple-A was moderate, nothing unusual, until the fighter pilots saw a SAM launch from their port side. It rose up in an arc headed for the AC-130. As the gunship rolled right to avoid the first SAM, two more were fired at it from different locations. There was no way out! They were bracketed.

The escort pilots agreed, she took a hit on the right wing inboard engine and an explosion and fire resulted. As the gunship started to drop down, another explosion occurred and something large and flaming separated from the aircraft.

"There was no mayday call," said the Phantom pilot.

"What about the beepers?" I asked him.

"We heard a couple very distinctly," he responded, "but all we could see down there in the darkness were fires on the ground."

My numbness intensified as Rhett and I wandered back to our revetment. Just as we rounded the corner, we witnessed the line truck unceremoniously pulling away with our ground power unit in tow. One side of the revetment cradled a lonely fire bottle, just like the one next to us. Otherwise the area was empty. The revetment suddenly looked huge and ghostly. We stood in silence for the longest time. I walked all around inside the revetment trying to wish my airplane back. Every stain, every tire mark had a sudden significance. It was eerie. I can't find the words to describe how we felt. I was hoping it was all a dream and our AC-130 would appear from around the corner, putting an end to all this. John and I realized we were forged together in tragedy. Ours is a bond that will last forever.

Search and rescue operations continued around the clock. Still, there was no word of any survivors. As the sun came up the next morning, the squadron commander asked both Sgt. Rhett and me to walk over to wing headquarters and with ceremony, lower the flag to half-mast. Spectre gunship tail number 55-0044 was the first AC-130 shot down by a surface-to-air missile. The date was March 29, 1972. I'll never forget.

As word spread across the flight line about the shoot down, we got another distress call. A second gunship was down! Aircraft No. 571 was flying just outside An Loc. That was Sgt. Wollman's plane! A small group of crew chiefs now gathered on the flight line. The line truck came rolling up.

"Where's Sgt. Wollman?" the driver asked.

"Today is his birthday, he's downtown celebrating," answered a chief from our group.

"Someone find him and bring him back here," ordered the driver as he sped away. One of the guys ran off to find Sgt. John Schrawder who was the assistant crew chief under Bob. Sergeant Schrawder knew where they could find Bob downtown and volunteered to get him. Meanwhile, another crew chief approached us. He said word had it the whole crew got out and were being picked up. This time there were survivors.

In one of the largest search and rescue operations of the war, all fourteen crewmen were picked up from the jungle and brought back to safety. Two AC-130 gunships had been lost within a few hours. Only one had a happy ending, and it wasn't mine. The call sign for my crew that night was "Spectre 13."

There was no time to mourn the loss of my crew as the North Vietnamese launched a massive attack on March 30th (now known as the Easter Offensive). This would soon be the largest enemy operation of the entire war, eclipsing the Tet Offensive of 1968. We were told Operation Commando Hunt VII was over; President Nixon ordered Operation Linebacker. The Air Force was now targeting North Vietnam's logistical networks and air bases. Our mission was to slow down the flow of men and materiel onto the battlefields and protect our assets. The enemy punctuated the opening moves of their offensive with the shooting down of a sophisticated gunship...mine.

John Rhett and I were reassigned to another aircraft. It was the sister ship to No. 044. My new gunship was No. 043. An "A" model, it preceded Zero Four Four off the assembly line back in 1955.

We went to work getting No. 043 ready to fly. The flight crews were very quiet when they came off the crew bus and boarded the aircraft. I did my walk-around with the pilot. He knew I was the crew chief on No. 044 and said it had been a good ship. As we finished our preflight, he shook my hand and promised to avenge the shoot-down of our friends. This was one time I wished I were going with them.

My anger and hatred were becoming all consuming. Now I wanted to know after each mission how many had paid the price. I quizzed the scanners about what they saw and did on the mission. "Did we produce secondary explosions?" I asked. "How many trucks tonight? Any troops found out in the open? How brutally did they die? Did you see any SAM's?" I was being sucked in....I could feel it but I couldn't seem to stop it. Nor did I want to.

I helped some of the gunners pack Smitty's personal belongings to send back to the States. I sat on a chair next to his bed, which someone had made up in proper military style. One of the scanners opened Smitty's locker and gently placed his personal items on his pillow. I got a shiver down my spine when I picked up his Zippo lighter. It finally hit me then that he was gone. All of Smitty's things were placed into a box and sealed up. They would be sent home to his next of kin. The process was repeated for the rest of the gunners: Todd, Simmons and Pearce. I was also on hand to help pack up Sergeant Caniford's personal things. This man was one of the most courageous IOs I ever met. I would miss his quick wit and his sense of what was right. My thoughts turned to Capt. Halpin. He wasn't supposed to even be on the plane and now he was MIA or dead. My anger continued to intensify over the loss and the waste.

One night I'm sitting alone and sulking, staring at my dinner in the NCO club dining room. From my left approached a very beautiful Thai girl. "Why you have sad eyes?" she asked standing near my table. I didn't realize it was that obvious to strangers and was taken aback by her question. Before I could conjure up an answer, she sat down across from me and continued, "You should be happy and smiling...not be sad. Yes?

My name…Malee [pronounced May-lee]. I am happy because I now have job here as new waitress. This is good for me and good for my family. You have family too…yes?"

"Yes, I have family back home." I replied.

"You miss family…this is why you sad?" she murmured.

"Yes I miss my family," I told her, "But that's not why I'm sad."

This sweet little Thai girl leaned in close from across the table and told me she had just gotten the word from the club manager that she was hired to be a waitress. Malee had apparently been trying for months for the job and only minutes ago given the opportunity. She was struck by the wide divide of emotions between us, and explained in her euphoria that she was compelled to stop and talk with me. I was surprised at her well-spoken English and her compassion for a stranger.

"My name is Tom," I told her, "I'm sad because I am a crew chief and I lost my airplane and crew a few days ago. They were shot down." This young girl looked deep into my eyes with a strange maturity and said, "We be friends so you not feel sad and alone." With that she reached across the table and held my hand. Her fingers entwined in mine felt so soft and delicate. I was honestly moved by her gesture and made no attempt to pull away. Malee and I sat for over an hour and talked about life, family, the war and Thailand. She either held or rubbed my hand the entire time and showed tremendous empathy for my emotions. I told her I now felt bad for bringing her down, but she insisted that was not the case and asked to meet me again. I heard myself making a date to see her again and she rushed outside to catch the Baht bus for home. Once I had finished my drink I wandered down to the post office to check for mail. Normally I would have sunk even lower seeing my empty box, but tonight I was under a spell. I made no mention to the guys back at our barracks of my encounter with Malee. As her fragrance and smile faded in my memory I began to think maybe this girl was just a clever Tee-lock looking for a new mark. I had to be careful not to be taken for a ride.

****

Back on the flight line our workload became even more strenuous and serious as flight operations intensified. Working on 043 was depressing since it was not in good shape. I found my mind wandering to Malee and her soft hands and soothing smile. Should I see her as planned or should I avoid her at all costs? Still not sure about my actions, I found myself having a solo dinner again at the club the next night. Malee was there and dressed in her new waitress outfit. She saw me as she came from the kitchen and walked directly to my table. "Hi Tom!" she purred. "You like my new dress?" twirling in a circle as she asked.

"Hi Malee. Yes, you look very nice." I told her. I meant every word, too. Standing beside this beautiful young girl I felt appreciated and warmed. She was even more beautiful than I remembered and the short skirt from her uniform only strengthened my feeling of attraction. "Stay after I finish work so we can talk. OK"? She winked as she asked. Not waiting for an answer, she spun around and danced away, moving with the music from the jukebox as she disappeared back into the kitchen. I was drawn to this young woman but still not sure of her intentions.

Later that night as she again sat at my table holding my hands, we explored all kinds of topics. I told her I was married with a daughter. She told me she lived with her older brother and her parents not far from the airbase. As I grew more comfortable with her I simply blurted out that I was not looking for a Tee-lock and didn't have the emotional strength to be taken advantage of. Malee seemed surprised I would suggest that was her motive. She was not upset that I brought it out in the open. She simply was excited to have her new job and knew part of that job was to be nice to the Americans and to expect they would try to take advantage of her. She seemed relieved that I was not in that category and we intuitively sat closer as we talked. I could feel her heat next to me as her thigh touched mine. Once the barriers came down we both opened up. I told her more about my home and family in the United States. She knew I was not a candidate for marriage and a free trip to the U.S. Still, this sweet young girl paid attention to my words and feelings and offered soothing advice and counsel. Much later, I walked her to the Baht bus and she gave me a hug before jumping onboard. Her long black hair whisked across my face as she spun away from our embrace.

Walking alone back to the barracks I felt both relieved and confused. Malee seemed genuine enough and her fragrance on my sleeve was intoxicating to be sure. Maybe that was the problem. I realized in a flash that I was falling in some way for this girl. Never mind she had a body to die for and those deep brown piercing eyes were mesmerizing. I was truly drawn by her soft expression of compassion. She used ideas and words that seemed beyond her nineteen years. The guys asked where I had been and I simply said the BX and a movie.

John Rhett and I sat around and listened to music on our headphones. As the music played my mind drifted to Malee. I was still depressed about losing my crew, but the feelings were tempered by the thought of seeing her again. Malee was becoming a pillar of strength and compassion. Yes, I was exploring feelings of passion as well. I was having a difficult time keeping her from my mind.

****

My new aircraft was in very poor condition. The previous crew chief had been the guy who tried to "butter" himself with the knife in the barracks a few weeks earlier. John and I continued to work on our new charge. Our top priority was to make it fly, which we did. During daylight hours we transformed No. 043 into a proud example of what an "A" model gunship should look and fly like. We cleaned and painted throughout the aircraft, both inside and out. We laid down new floor covering in the booth and on the flight deck. What had been a drab and dreary machine was transformed into something admirable; at least we thought so.

Very quickly we had no time for appearances. The North Vietnamese were swarming all over South Vietnam, and Spectre was getting the call for help. Our black gunships were flying daylight missions now and it was all we could do to get them armed, fueled, repaired and launched. Then, we had to do it all over a few hours later, and again and again. Nights were becoming days and days were nights. I never knew what day of the week it was; it didn't matter. We worked, it seemed, around the clock to keep them up in the air. If mine were in the air, I would be helping John Forsberg or someone else with their aircraft. Now we were getting calls from Americans in jeopardy—Pleiku, Kontum, Dak To, An Loc and Quang Tri to name a few places. Spectre was kept in the air and in the fight by the overwhelming efforts of her many 16th SOS ground crewmen.

Forsberg's newly repaired and equipped 105mm gunship rose above the rest of our AC-130s in the squadron. This Spectre could knock out a tank with one shot! In fact, Captain Olson's crew did that and more over Dak To one night by taking out seven enemy tanks.

****

Another gunship was hit! A hand-held Strela missile struck this one. The missile hit the aircraft right next to the infrared light and passed through the outer skin, exploding in the rear cargo area above where the IO lay. The aircraft and crew made it to a base in South Vietnam. No one had been seriously hurt. The crew chief flew out the next morning to retrieve his battle damaged gunship.

****

The large number of high-caliber enemy guns along the Trail, required that our aircraft fly at a higher altitude. This usually meant our 7.62mm and 20mm guns were less effective. We started loading extra 40mm ammo and less of the small stuff. This season we had a relatively new type of 40mm shell. It was called "misch-metal." These shells contained phosphorous, would burn at extreme temperatures and would explode and set fire to anything! My crew would return with tales of flaming destruction. I began to eagerly embrace the havoc.

Now my Spectre gunship was lighting up the sky, day and night. The enemy was paying a heavy price. The carnage continued unabated. The aircrews were weary, but they kept at it. We all did. History will show that American air power stemmed the tide. It was through hard work and dedication that the few Americans that were in Southeast Asia at the time, were able to do just that.

The F-4 squadrons at Ubon were also flying around the clock. More and more of them came limping back with battle damage as well. Since all the gunships were in the air now we didn't have 130s to stand on top of, to watch the jets come crashing in.

Our AC130s began flying orbits around Ubon's perimeter before and after missions in Laos. They used the white searchlight to light up the area and discourage sappers. We thought it was a pretty cool light show as well.

Extra units came in from the Philippines, Japan and the United States under Operation Constant Guard. Suddenly the grass fields we rode our bikes through months before were becoming tent cities with all the new personnel arriving. The level of activity at the base rose ten-fold. In the middle of it all, I kept my new gunship in the air and part of the fight. I still mourned for the loss of my crew. Actually, I kept hoping they would walk out of the jungle and appear on the base perimeter.

We didn't have time anymore for our usual rounds of poker with the other gunners and scanners. Now, they were either flying or fast asleep. We were working tirelessly day and night on our aircraft (sometimes sleeping in the gunship itself). I listened again to the audio tape and was haunted by some of the voices of my downed crew.

I continued to share my thoughts and feelings with Malee at the club whenever possible. She acted like "my girl" whenever I would enter the club. I felt good when she would leave a table full of GIs just to come across the room to greet me. She made me feel quite special that way, and I could see the looks of envy in the eyes of the young Airmen competing for her attention. Ours had become a special bond tethered by our initial meeting when I was so "down" and she was so "up."

One night, Malee invited me to her parent's house. "I want you meet my mother and father," she announced. "Don't worry it mean nothing beyond that." She laughed, sensing my hesitation. "I think my brother want to check you out," she added with a sly smile.

Two nights later I met Malee at the bus stop and we rode the short distance to her parent's house. Their home was like most there, raised up on stilts and open to the elements. I followed Malee up the stairs and removed my shoes as she did just before entering the bungalow. In Thai she spoke first to her father and then to her mother. They said something in return then offered a nice greeting in English. "Welcome, Tom, to our home," Malee's father said, grasping my hand and then bowing. He was short but appeared very strong and his skin was weathered from years of working the fields. Her mother was small in stature and dressed in a silk gown of some kind. I bowed in respect to both parents as we adjourned to the next room. I was surprised at the near fluent English spoken by both parents, and felt a little embarrassed when I tried to speak Thai with them. They laughed gently and seemed to understand my difficulty. I told them I had no special designs on their daughter and that she was more like a spiritual guide who found me at just the right time. Halfway through our meal of rice and fish, Malee's brother arrived. For a Thai he was built strong and stood a little taller than most. I shook his hand and bowed in respect. He said something in Thai to Malee and her parents, then sat down next to me at the table. It turns out her brother also worked at the base and was quite familiar with the AC-130s. He worked the wash rack last year and had recently been promoted to work in one of the large base warehouses. His English was not as good as the others, so he kept reverting back to Thai. I was pleased when his father reprimanded him for being discourteous in front of their English-speaking guest. I felt the same warmth and compassion from Malee's parents as I had from her.

After our meal her brother sat on one side of me and Malee on the other as we sipped a cool lemon drink on their porch. After twenty minutes or so her brother stood up and said, "Tom, I like you. I love my sister... I not want to see her hurting." I promised him I was not about to hurt her and was simply her very good friend. He said something again in Thai to Malee then shook my hand. He bowed once more and left the room. "We go for a walk?" suggested Malee. I finished my drink and stood up helping Malee to stand with my outstretched hand.

While walking in the cool night air, Malee told me I had been accepted by her family; even her brother seemed to like me. I told her she was lucky to have such nice parents and how pleased I was that they in turn liked me. We walked and talked holding hands as we strolled along the now darkened street. She looked so radiant in her yellow flowered dress.

Her smooth skin accentuated by the bright white of her sandals and a multi-colored bracelet on her right wrist. Coming around the corner near her home, Malee suddenly stopped and started to tremble. This took me completely by surprise. She nestled in my outstretched arms and said, "Tom, you mean more to me than I can talk about. I know we have no future together... you married and have family. Most GIs on base try only to get Malee in bed, but you not try to kiss me." She paused a moment and looked me in the eyes whispering, "You make me want you more." Her eyes showed tears even in the darkness as she bared her soul to me. I pulled her in closer and held her in my arms for a moment. I could feel her heart beating next to mine as I soothed her long hair in my fingers. Neither of us spoke for what seemed like a long time.

Then with a move of her hand across her face to clear her hair, Malee lifted up on her toes and softly but passionately kissed me full on the lips. Her kiss sent electric currents through my body. I was astounded by her display of affection. I stood in the middle of the dark and deserted road and kissed her again. Honestly it wasn't sex on my mind. I was feeling a close personal bond that I had not felt in months and something I so desperately needed to feel right then. This simple yet stunningly beautiful girl had turned my sorrow and grief into a sense of new hope and affection. I walked her to her bungalow and she held me for a long while and said nothing. We didn't feel the need for verbal conversation. Somewhere in the distance we could hear a stereo playing a song by Buffalo Springfield called "For What It's Worth." We swayed gently to the music, slow dancing right in the middle of the street. I kissed her long and passionately.

Releasing her long enough to gather my composure, I told her I had to catch the next bus back to base. She asked me to come to the NCO club the following Thursday and wait for her. "I have surprise for you," was all she said. I held her in my arms and kissed her again. "I'll wait for you in the dining room," I said as I backed away from her embrace. I watched her walk to the top of her stairs and, after removing her sandals, disappear inside.

"What am I doing?" I kept asking myself that question as I walked to the bus stop. The bus was half empty, and the only passengers were GIs heading back to base from a night out or some in uniform heading to work. No one seemed to have missed me once back in the barracks. I knew I couldn't tell my friends about my evening. Still, I couldn't stop thinking about Malee and knew I would be awaiting her surprise come Thursday.

****

I needed new tools. My tool box with a full complement of tools and my journal all went down in flames with No. 044. I tried to explain that to the sergeant in charge of the tool crib. He just didn't seem to get the picture. He acted like the sergeant back at Dyess when John Forsberg and I broke the truck door. He was concerned about my disregard for government property. Our argument became heated, and I told him if he needed his tools that badly, then run over to Laos and start searching. They were probably spread over a mile or two of jungle. I think he finally got the point. However, the sticky part was I had to ask this sergeant if I could check out *another* tool box. His jaw dropped when I brought it up, and all he did was point to the door.

****

Now, every night and every day our planes flew missions returning to us only to refuel and rearm before we sent them up again. Black gunships in daylight are not hard to spot. Spectre was fighting both in and out of its element. We took more hits as a result. We hit the enemy harder! John Rhett and I redoubled our efforts to keep 043 flying and in the fight.

Early one morning when 043 came in to refuel and rearm, I talked with the scanner about what was happening out there. They had been helping to defend a fortification against human wave attacks. He said they would make a pass and drop the enemy at the barbed wire, then, as they came around again, they saw the VC crawling over their comrades' bodies. "So we'd hose 'em down too," he said, only to repeat the process over and over. They were literally "stacking 'em up too high to crawl over," he continued. I tried to imagine what lay before this man's eyes only an hour before and most probably what he would be returning to again once I had finished. If only they could find the missile sites that took out my aircraft, I'd be happy.

I finished up and we went through engine start-up and launch. As I had each time before, I proudly saluted the pilot and offered him the thumbs up as I sent him towards the runway. This young pilot saluted back with a smile and gave me the peace sign! I never saw him again. No, he didn't crash that night. I did.

The maintenance chief found me at the flight line snack bar. Something was said about those early outs we had requested a month or so ago. All he said was, "You better get packing."

About forty of us had signed on for early outs and a large group of us were now in our barracks packing. We were told to grab essentials and that the squadron would see to it the rest of our stuff got home. John Forsberg promised to watch over all our belongings. He had not been eligible yet for the early out, so he would not be leaving. All of this was happening so fast I had forgotten what day it was. Of course, it was Thursday.

"Wait! I'm supposed to see Malee tonight!" I said to myself. I had most of my stuff packed and on my bed when I jumped on the bike downstairs and rode to the NCO club. I knew Malee would be hurt and disappointed that I was leaving but I HAD to say goodbye. I entered the cool air-conditioned club for the last time and scoured the room for her. I grabbed a nearby waitress and asked her if she knew Malee. "Yes," she said, "but she no here yet." I tried to quickly explain my situation but the girl was busy and only responded by saying, "Maybe you come back later." I had no time to spare and had to ride back to my barracks to await our orders.

Before I knew it, we were being taken by the Spectre wagon down to the squadron. This trailer was a carnival type wagon, pulled by a jeep. It was reserved for only Spectre personnel. At Spectre Operations, we were given chromed 40mm shells with our names on them. They told us to pin on a Presidential Unit Citation Award, the Vietnamese Gallantry Cross with Palm and a few others. We were then whisked to the air terminal to await our flights... *Wait a minute, what did they mean flights in the plural? Weren't we all heading to the same place...home?* The answer, of course, was no!

John Rhett and about twenty others went to Korat in Southern Thailand. The rest of us would be going northeast to Nakhon Phanom (NKP).

"Are we going to the States from there?" someone asked. No one seemed to know. So we said our goodbyes there in the terminal at Ubon and got on C-130s as passengers for a trip into the unknown. Since I had not told anyone about Malee I couldn't expect them to find her and explain what was happening. My initial rush of euphoria over going home was replaced by the empty cold feeling of leaving this sweet young girl without explanation. Before she started her shift at the club, I realized, I'll be miles away. By the time she gives up waiting for me, I'll be processed in and assigned to a new squadron at a new air base over a hundred miles away.

As if all this going on wasn't bizarre enough, the day just happened to be a national holiday in Thailand, called the "Songkran Festival." Also known as "The Water Festival," this holiday is the traditional Thai New Year and water fights represent the celebration of the holiday. It starts with squirt guns and water balloons, then on to fire hoses and buckets. We were drenched in our ride around the base on the Spectre wagon. As we were receiving our accolades at Squadron Operations, we were all dripping wet. At the flight terminal, as we said goodbye to each other, John Forsberg doused the Spectre squadron commander with a bucket of water. The commander was shocked, but took it in stride. It was just so typical of Forsberg. He was a great, great friend! I never saw him again after that day, April 13, 1972. We didn't know it at the time, but our little trio ended that day. John Forsberg, John Rhett and I stood together for the last time for a photo with our still wet squadron commander. In the photo, John Rhett is seen holding a pistol in his hand, waiting for anything. Of course, it was a water pistol.

Sergeant Rhett ended up working on the Airborne Command and Control Aircraft at Korat Air Base. Their C-130s contained the latest communications equipment and would orbit above an area for long periods of time, coordinating the actions below. I did not see John Rhett again until we both left the Air Force and returned to Washington. To this day, he remains a very good friend.

The crew chief on the C-130 that took us to NKP would not permit any display of water sports on his aircraft. I admired him for that. I was dripping wet but I managed to keep my dad's treasured camera dry. Treasured, because he was an avid film buff and took great pride in his camera equipment. Dad had died only a few years before and his camera was one of a few things he left me that allowed me to feel close to him.

I gazed out the porthole window waving a silent goodbye to the world as I had known it for the last six months. I had made many friends there and while some saw me depart, many others could not. We were deprived of handshakes, friendly wishes and fond memories. They would arrive on the flight line to start preflight and be told of those of us who were sent away and why. At least they would know what had become of us.

The entire six months at Ubon came at me in a rush: The possibility of flying as an IO and the battle damage to Zero Four Four; the months of hard and hot work repairing our ship. The friends made, the courage I witnessed in my flight crews. The battle damage on friends' aircraft, and the hours spent repairing. The F-4s constant take offs and sometimes heroic landings. The loss of my beloved airplane and crew. The irony of Wollman's gunship lost with all onboard saved only hours after my crew was hit. The loss of my innocence and the funk that only a young Thai girl named Malee noticed and tried to mend.

I regret that I never got the chance to say a true and proper goodbye to Malee. The fact that I stood her up and left without as much as a "see ya'" burned in my chest. She deserved better and I can only hope that in time she would have heard about the group of Spectres that were shipped out in a hurry, and realized I had to have been one of them. I hope she knew me well enough to know I would not simply stop seeing her without explanation. Maybe she felt the kisses and tender moments scared me away? What was the surprise that she treasured to share with me? It will always be a shame I could not say farewell to that sweet and lovely girl. Deep down, however, I knew it was the best course of action. I was still quite married, of course, and was now being pulled away from a very strong temptation. "I sure could use Dad's guidance now," I thought as we rumbled along in silence. We flew Northward with little or no conversation. Most of us had to be feeling the same way after being rushed out of town like that.

The C-130 droned on for some time before we heard the familiar sounds of the landing gear coming down. I felt as low as I had in the past half-year. In fact, I was feeling absolutely dismal.

On the other hand if we were rotating back to the World after a quick stop over at NKP... I would certainly welcome that.

TEN

Nakhon Phanom

"**W**ELCOME TO THE 23RD TACTICAL AIR SUPPORT SQUADRON, home to the Nail OV-10 Bronco. My name is Sgt. Jones and I'm here to help you with your in-processing." The young sergeant walked around the room, collecting our orders as he spoke. We were gathered in the orderly room of the 56th Special Operations Wing, Nakhon Phanom, Thailand (NKP). For a stunned moment, the only sound came from the steady hum of the over-used air conditioner.

"I think there has been some mistake here Sarge," someone from our group said. "We're supposed to get early outs to rotate back to the World."

"There is no mistake," he said, "you're here to finish out your tours before rotating back. Blame the North Vietnamese—they're the ones who launched a new offensive."

We'd been had! I had a feeling something like this was going to happen. I remembered the old saying in the military about not volunteering for anything. I would have preferred to stay at Ubon and the 16th SOS if we had to finish out our tours. It was too late. We would be assigned to the flight line and the Bronco OV-10s.

Nakhon Phanom was now my new home.

The guys from our group were assigned to specific shops. Some went to avionics or the machine shop and others to administrative positions. Only a few of us would be put back on the flight line.

We were assigned rooms and given directions to find them. Our new barracks were the old hooch style, like I had "enjoyed" originally at Ubon. They were not air-conditioned. Our barracks were close to those of the "Zorros" and a detachment of the "Night Owls." In fact, we were right next door to their hooch bar. One of the guys explained to us that the Zorros flew the A-1 Skyraider in support of search and rescue operations. The Owls flew night missions.

We quickly became settled in our new home. A couple of other Spectre crew chiefs shared the new room with me. Again, we moved lockers around to create a living space. I picked a top bunk and moved it directly under a ceiling fan. One way or another, I was going to cool down. I had to be careful...if I sat upright in my bunk I'd receive a haircut! Once we were settled in, a few of us decided to wander around the base to get acquainted with the layout. We were housed in barracks that sat far away from the flight line and right on the perimeter of the base.

Noticing our Spectre hats, some of the Zorros invited us into their hooch bar where they gave us beer and soda, "on the house." We were welcome to come back anytime, the pilots told us. The reason, of course, was because we were standing in front of the very guys that had flown the rescue operations for our two Spectre gunships! They were equally surprised to learn that I was the crew chief to the first aircraft. Their condolences were replaced with pride however when we talked of the second shoot-down. Obviously these guys felt the joy of a successful pick-up of downed crewmembers and equally the sorrow of no survivors. The pilots had many questions about our AC-130s. I felt a surge of pride when I spoke of my lost gunship and the others of Spectre.

About an hour later, we wandered over to check out the NCO club. It wasn't as nice as the one we had left behind at Ubon. Of course the floor of the entire club was a half-inch deep in water. The flood was the result of the still on-going Songkran Festival. There was a brand new Base Exchange, located next to the much smaller and older Exchange. We quickly noticed NKP had two theaters as well, one inside and the other outdoors. The amphitheater was dedicated to pilots lost in battle. We roamed the base for a while, avoiding the water balloons being tossed from passing cars. Eventually we made our way to the flight line. I noticed that Air Police were stationed along the Nail OV-10 hangers in sentry posts. Security here was tight, much the same as Ubon. We attracted attention wearing our Spectre hats and that made me proud.

The next morning we checked in at the 23rd TASS Operations Center located next to the flight line. The 23rd was one squadron in the 56th Special Operations Wing and was responsible for maintaining and flying the OV-10 Bronco aircraft.

Next to the door leading into the Ops center was a large squadron patch. The 23rd was home to the Cricket. The patch showed Jiminy Cricket suspended under his umbrella, holding a radio and pointing to the ground. A sergeant entering the building noticed me staring at the patch. "Walt Disney studios designed it," he said as he walked by.

Once inside the building, the Ops officer informed us that the call sign "Nail" had been implemented. We were given the rundown on the squadron's mission and how we fit in.

The more I heard about the 23rd Tass and what the squadron had accomplished, the more impressed I became. I quickly learned that these guys were Air Commando all the way! The brotherhood of Special Ops was evident by our reception from the OV-10 pilots especially. However, the Operations officer surprised me when he introduced those of us who had just come up from Spectre. He singled me out as the crew chief from the first AC-130 shot down last month. These guys all had been a part of the large dual rescues just weeks earlier and now they too offered their condolences. I was just slightly overwhelmed. We had various maintenance briefings for the next few hours; then we were all turned loose. Walking out of the Operations shed together, one of the pilots offered me an up-close view of his OV-10.

The Bronco was a small two-seat aircraft used primarily as a FAC or Forward Air Control. It had a fighter-style cockpit for two in tandem, and was powered by two turboprop jet engines. The props were counter-rotating for stability. It was equipped with four 7.62mm machine guns. The OV-10 used a twin boom configuration to a high horizontal stabilizer in back. It was a mean looking little aircraft.

A blue Air Force truck slowly approached us coming to a stop next to our OV-10. I was introduced to the line chief. The chief said the 23rd TASS was currently involved in retrofitting the OV-10s with laser designators, under the code names "Pave Nail" and "Pave Spot." This would mean among other things, the OV-10s could be used to "paint" targets for the F-4 Phantoms instead of the Spectre gunships. The line chief was quite pleased to have former Spectre ground crew who understood the system as part of his squadron. I was assigned to the phase hangar. This meant I would not be a crew chief on any one aircraft, but would be involved with the retrofit program for the whole squadron.

I was introduced to the folks in the phase hangar and by the second day, issued another toolbox. I was given a proper run-through on the various systems of the OV-10. The line chief cautioned me numerous times to avoid the eject mechanisms in the cockpit. One of the crew chiefs offered to give me a tour of the flight line as well. He soon grabbed a tug and away we went.

Among the many missions provided by the Air Force at NKP, the dominant role was that of Search and Rescue (SAR). Along with the OV-10 aircraft, the base housed the A-1 Skyraiders, a squadron of AC-119 Stinger gunships and HH-53 Jolly Green helicopters (code name "Knife"). The Jolly Greens were used not only to retrieve downed airmen, but also for clandestine operations day or night. "Those Jollys over there," said the chief, "were some of the ones used in the Son Tay raid over a year ago." The crew chief was referring to the secret mission to rescue American POWs. All went mostly according to plan, except the POWs were gone! Our guys shot up the camp and a nearby enemy barracks before departing the area.

NKP was a secret staging base for Special Operation inserts into Laos, Cambodia and North Vietnam. Movement around the Knife helicopters was closely monitored by fatigue clad Air Police carrying M-16s. The A-1s were called "Sandys" by their pilots. They typically were used to soften up an area around a downed pilot before the Jolly Greens arrived. Further down the line was a detachment of EC-47 aircraft as well. Air Police patrolled the entire area. The flight line was an interesting place.

Right away I noticed by working in the small open-ended hangars, I was out of the direct heat of the sun. The flight line was made of steel interlocking planks called PSP (Pierced Steel Planks). It absorbed the intense heat during the day, and was slippery when wet from rain or hydraulic fluid. The average temperature was probably 98 degrees or so in the shade.

I was depressed that we did not get our early outs and that I had left most of my friends, including Malee, at Ubon. I also missed working on and preparing my new gunship, No. 043. I was happy about one thing, though. I no longer was participating in death and destruction, but rather with search and rescue. Instead of taking lives we'd be saving them...or so I thought.

My first full week working with the 23rd TASS was dominated by its participation in the rescue of BAT-21. Lieutenant Colonel Hambleton was a navigator on board an EB-66 aircraft, call sign BAT-21. The EB-66 was escorting a group of B-52 bombers on a mission near the DMZ. Three SAM missiles were fired at the EB-66. (The same tactic used to shoot down my gunship.) Hambleton was the only one in the crew of six to bail out of the stricken aircraft. One of our OV-10 Nail aircraft was able to pinpoint the survivor. A rescue attempt using Hueys and Cobra gunships resulted in the loss of one Huey and crew, plus heavy damage to the other aircraft. On the second day of the operation, a hand-held SA-2 Strela missile shot down one of our OV-10s (call sign Nail-38). Both pilot and copilot (Captain Henderson and Lieutenant Clark) ejected. Henderson was captured. The copilot was down close to Lt. Col. Hambleton's position. They both called in air strikes, dangerously close at times, on the enemy all around them. On the next attempt to pick up the remaining two pilots, an HH-53 (call sign Jolly Green 67) was shot down. All on board were lost.

Hambleton and Clark were down on the ground in the middle of a major battle. They were surrounded by thousands of enemy troops, tanks, artillery and air defense guns. United States FACs, fighters and rescue craft were all suffering battle damage. SAM missiles were being fired in unprecedented numbers. Another OV-10 was shot down, this one from the 20th Tass stationed at Da Nang. Only one of the pilots came up on the radio. He was farther away from Bat-21 and Nail-38. Another SAR was scrambled to find and rescue him. Unfortunately, days later he was shot while evading and was not rescued.

The two remaining pilots evaded capture and were finally picked up by Navy Seals after almost two weeks on the ground. I had been with the squadron only a short time and already the people here were making news. I realized I had traded one specialized outfit for another. (Years later, the story of BAT-21 would be made into a movie, although not a very accurate one.)

The enemy offensive was massive on all scales. The North was attempting to swiftly occupy and capture all of South Vietnam. North Vietnamese regulars came pouring down from the DMZ, as well as from their sanctuaries in Laos and Cambodia. The enemy had tanks on the move and large caliber weapons flowing south. We already knew they had SAMs and rockets. With the loss of one of our Broncos to a Strela missile, we knew the stakes were now higher.

The pressure was on to get our OV-10s outfitted with the new electronics and back into the air. Numerous times, I stopped to wipe the sweat from my hands, my brow and the wrench I was using. The air was stagnant with jet fuel and hydraulic fluid. I wore a bandanna around my head to keep the drops of sweat from my eyes. Some of the lifers didn't like the way I looked with the multicolored bandanna...tough shit. I was "asked" to see the captain about it, so I went to visit the young officer in his air-conditioned trailer one afternoon. We came to an agreement: I could continue to wear a bandanna, only not one with colors. He said I could wear olive green or white. I was prepared to do battle with the captain, because he didn't have to work on hot aircraft all day in the heat. But surprisingly he understood. He wasn't wearing wings, so he was not a flyer. If he were a pilot, we wouldn't be talking about such bullshit. Pilots understood what we endured. They trusted their lives to us every time they strapped in. The last thing they wanted to worry about as they flew into combat was whether or not the aircraft is reliable. Pilots were our allies. To my surprise, so was this captain.

The offensive bandanna, multicolored, with the word "Vietnam" on the front, was packed away. It was a gift from a fellow crew chief. When his OV-10 crash-landed at Da Nang, he flew in from NKP to do repairs. I had told him to bring back a souvenir. Months later, his bird crash-landed again at Da Nang. To this day, I have both colorful bandannas!

****

One day we heard the familiar sirens of the fire trucks as they raced to the runway. We watched as a crippled OV-10 came in to attempt a landing. Just before touching down, the aircraft banked sharply to the right, putting the right wing tip to the ground. The pilot and copilot ejected, but they flew sideways instead of up. They impacted the ground near the perimeter. The OV-10 did a rapid cartwheel before exploding beside the runway. Both pilots perished. I didn't know either of them; however, the crew chief was stricken and we all tried to console him. *I couldn't handle losing more friends*, I thought. The flag was lowered to half-mast by someone over at Wing headquarters. Everyone's mood was somber after that. Our task was to keep 'em flying, so we went back to doing our jobs, but nothing was quite the same again.

****

We got word of an F-4 pilot out of Udorn that was shot down by a MIG. He was in North Vietnam. We were given daily updates on his movements. He evaded capture for over three weeks before being picked up by the Jolly Greens. We gathered around the giant rescue helicopter as it landed near our hangar. I saw Captain Locher step down from the Jolly Green and kiss the ground, happy to be alive! Someone handed him a beer as everyone crowded around him. He shook hands with the air crew and was whisked away.

****

As we continued to crank out our Pave-Nail OV-10s, the air war grew with intensity. Now the OV-10 pilots were returning with success stories, applauding the new equipment. Seeing my Spectre hat, a few of them related stories of successful missions in support of the gunships. Our

Pave-Nail OV-10s were locating and targeting SAM sites for the F-4 Phantoms as well. I felt as if finally we were striking back at those who were hurting us the most. I wanted retribution for the loss of my aircraft and crew. My efforts were paying off. We worked long and hard to get our Broncos outfitted and into the air.

I became very familiar with the systems of the OV-10s. On occasion, I would help launch and recover them on the flight line. The pilots were always friendly and fair, usually offering advice and explaining their problems with the aircraft.

I met Lt. Clark one afternoon as he strapped into his gray OV-10. He was a quiet unassuming guy and a true warrior. Everyone on base had heard of his exploits with BAT-21 and no one expected him to fly combat again. But here he was, ready to continue the fight. These guys were tough!

After "owning" a large aircraft like a C-130, maintaining a small airplane such as the OV-10 was relatively simple. It was a reliable aircraft. The systems were straightforward and we enjoyed easy access to most all its components. Besides, I had good teachers there in the 23rd Tass.

****

One of our former Spectre chiefs was a stocky blond named Fred Marshall. Fred was now the crew chief of an OV-10. One day while we were preflighting his aircraft, Fred happened to mention his hooch had an extra bunk, and I was invited in. His barracks were of the same configuration but were located closer to the flight line and high on a hill. I was eager to get away from the perimeter. Trip flares were going off nightly. Another prior Spectre crew chief, Dan O'Neill was situated there as well. Dan, like most of us, was not happy to be there. He was very outspoken with the lifers about the injustice done to us. Of course, it fell on deaf ears. Still, Sgt. O'Neill was a good spokesman for our group, as he'd SAY what we actually FELT. He was not afraid to stand up to authority either. Together we had that bond of owning and repairing battle damaged aircraft.

Before we left Ubon, Sgt. O'Neill and others patched up 509 just enough allowing it to be flown Stateside for major structural repairs. He finished the job just before my gunship was lost. Dan and Fred Marshall had been good friends back at Ubon. Now, our small group of crew chiefs merged together to finish out our tours.

****

NKP was located about 150 miles northeast of Ubon and right on the border with Laos. This area was more dangerous than Ubon. We were about seventy-five miles from the North Vietnamese Air Base at Vinh. It was not unusual to actually get Mig alerts from time to time. Directly east across Laos was North Vietnam! The Ho Chi Minh Trail was less than fifty miles away. Like Laos and Cambodia, Thailand was neutral, but try explaining that to the VC. The VC wanted to destroy the airplanes, but they also were after the sophisticated radar networks housed at NKP.

I moved in with Fred up on the hill. After work, at night, he and I would sit on our hooch steps and watch the "Arc Light" missions over the Ho Chi Minh Trail. Arc Light was the code name for B-52 bombing missions. From our vantage point it looked and sounded like a very big thunder and lightning storm. Passing a joint back and forth, we could see the flash and hear the roar as the bombs exploded in the distance. On occasion, we could see the streaking exhaust of a SAM missile as it rose in the night sky. It was surreal.

I had been there about a month and had not left the base. We were told about an OV-10 crew chief that went alone to downtown Nakhon Phanom, about ten miles from our base. He was never heard from again. We were cautioned not to go anywhere off base alone. I planned to stay right there, close to the flight line and our hooch area.

At the Base Exchange, I bought a Seiko watch like most air and ground crews had. It became another symbol of our elite fraternity. I still have it today, locked away like so many memories.

Fred took me to the base *dojo* (training hall) to watch his karate class. He was a brown belt and had taken classes back at Ubon. He and Sgt. Wollman had worked out together and became close friends. I mentioned the Seattle connection and the fact that Bob and I had both lost our gunships to enemy fire. On occasion, I watched Fred work out in class but decided not to join. The routine seemed too "military" at the time, and the instructor was very strict and demanding. Fred and I usually talked about martial arts for long periods, usually over a meal or back at the hooch area.

In the privacy of our hooch, he would demonstrate. "Hit me," he'd say. I would casually loft a left jab or a right. Fred would respond with lightning speed each time. If I tried to swing my fists harder or faster at him it made no difference. He would block me and launch an attack with his hands and feet, "tapping" me numerous times in the blink of an eye! Each move was landing less than an inch away! I was dumbfounded. As the months passed by, Fred continued to teach me this move or that. With each lesson my respect grew dramatically. I would have to credit him with lighting a fire deep inside me. Today, I hold the black belt rank of Go-Dan (5th degree) in Go-ju style karate. Fred, wherever you are…thank you!

****

Our maintenance chief was a lifer and a real hard-ass. No one liked him. He sat in his air-conditioned office and smoked his pipe and barked orders day after day. Someone suggested sprinkling a little marijuana in his tin can of tobacco. We all laughed at the suggestion. A few weeks later, the chief mellowed out. He was warm and receptive, and actually started telling us jokes. We all looked at each other knowingly and smiled. No, I didn't do it…but I know who did!

****

One afternoon just after towing another OV-10 into our hangar, we heard a tremendous explosion. Everyone ran outside and over to the hangar next door. I was not prepared for what I saw. An OV-10 crew chief while working in the rear cockpit of his plane had pulled the ejection handle by mistake. He was hurled up through the roof of the hangar. The seat landed 100 yards away. There was a large jagged hole in the roof of the hangar. The OV-10 was damaged as well. They found the crew chief 's mangled body just outside the back of the hangar. His war was over.

We discussed again the hazards of the eject handles. They had safety streamers to alert us to their proximity. However, the cockpit was small and working in it was difficult at best. There was not much room for error, obviously.

****

On a rare evening off while sitting in our hooch, Fred opened his locker and proudly showed me a large bag of marijuana. It was probably a few pounds at least. He said anytime I wanted some to just open his locker and take it. He gave me the combination to his lock. Sometimes Fred and I, along with some of the other crew chiefs, would walk along the deserted perimeter road at night and light up. Looking back, we would have made great targets if a sniper was in the trees. Usually afterwards we would head over to the NCO club for a meal or to the theater to take in a movie. We tried the outdoor theater one night and found it enjoyable. It was like a drive-in theater without the cars. We sat on benches and could listen through the numerous speakers scattered around. I remember the first movie we watched there was "Easy Rider." One side of our audience was full of lifers and red necks while another was filled with "heads." The movie was about bigotry and prejudice in the American South. Each time something happened to the "hippies" on screen, the lifers would hoot and howl in drunken concert. Just like the movie, the lines were being drawn right there in the jungle.

Soon we were driven from the outdoor theater to anything indoors— the monsoons had arrived. Being from the Northwest, I was used to seeing rain. I wasn't used to seeing it pour down like that. The rain came down so hard that I couldn't see ten feet in front of me!

On the hill, in the center of our group of hooches, was our squadron's hooch bar. We had a pool table and a long bar set up inside. During the rains I would venture only as far as the hooch bar. Here, I could get a beer or a Coke along with a sandwich. To walk any farther meant a complete drenching. Unfortunately, the walk to the flight line was about two blocks. I was usually soaked by the time I got to my hangar. We began stashing spare uniforms in the hangar to change into.

Sometimes, it was a wet disappointment to make the trek to the post office in the rain, only to find my box empty. On the other hand, if I had mail, it would be the highlight of my day. Mail from home was my only link with the sanity of the "normal" world. On occasion, I would receive an audio tape from family. I would listen to their voices over and over, yearning to be with them. I had changed from the young man they had last seen months before. Just how different had I become? The sweet sound of Tracy's voice in that little machine could bring tears to my eyes. The whole family would laugh and joke, sounding their usual carefree selves. I felt light-years away from "carefree." Their attempts were to cheer me up, I know, but sometimes it had the opposite effect.

****

Another OV-10 crew chief moved into our hooch. His name was Sparky. We decided to move the lockers and two bunk beds to one side and with a curtain divide the room into living and sleeping quarters. We put posters up on the walls of our "living room" and had old wood crates to house our stereo gear. The only problem was we didn't have any curtains.

Sparky and I decided upon a shopping trip downtown to Nakhon Phanom. We took a harrowing taxi ride the ten miles or so to the town. It was somewhat smaller than Ubon and much less friendly. Sparky and I went to a few dreary shops, with pesky shoeshine boys following us along the way. The town was dirty and dusty. We picked up a few items, including some black cloth for our curtains. We ate lunch at a little cafe on the Mekong River. Directly across the river was Thakhet, Laos. Thakhet was a known stronghold of the Pathet Lao and we could plainly see the soldiers working out in the hot sun within their compound.

After lunch, Sparky and I endured the rough taxi ride back to base. The taxi driver seemed to enjoy our discomfort and took greater risks to intensify it. He thought nothing of passing on hills or around corners. Perhaps as Americans, we had worn out our welcome. Or, perhaps these guys were just shitty drivers. Anyway, once safely back on base, we set up our curtains and presto, we now had living quarters!

One night Fred and I were sitting in our hooch listening to music when

Sparky burst into the room. "You've gotta' hear this," he exclaimed, pulling a record from its sleeve. Without saying who it was, he put the record on the turntable and cranked up the volume. I was blown away! It was "Stairway To Heaven" by Led Zeppelin. Fred lit up a joint and passed it around. We listened to the album over and over. Suddenly, there was a pounding on our door. I got up and pushed it open only to find an Air Police officer standing there. He was holding a large dog on a leash. I figured we were all busted. Instead, he and his German shepherd entered the room and simply asked us to turn down the music. With that, he turned around and left!

****

Back on the flight line, the pace was nonstop. The North Vietnamese were swarming all across Laos and South Vietnam. More and more OV-10s returned with small caliber bullet holes. The sheet metal shop was given the task of patching the holes. To move the OV-10s to their shop, we merely hooked up the small tug and towed the aircraft to another hangar. I began to enjoy driving the tug. Bouncing along the PSP that made up our flight line, I would stop and chat with the crew chiefs of the A-1 Sandys or the HH-53 helicopters.

One day I noticed an AC-119K Stinger aircraft sitting in a hangar. The C-119 was known as the flying boxcar. In terms of armament, it was a step up from the AC-47 "Spooky" aircraft (also known as "Puff the Magic Dragon"), but not nearly as sophisticated or powerful as the AC-130s. Only a few AC-119s remained and had been turned over to the Vietnamese Air Force.

I got off my tug and wandered over to the large black aircraft. No one was around, so I entered the gunship. It was equipped with four of the 7.62mm mini-guns and two, 20mm Gatling guns. The rest of the cargo area was filled with sophisticated electronics similar to the Spectre AC-130s. There was no booth. Now having come from Spectre, I was spoiled, but this was some lethal machine! I would be proud to be a crew chief on this aircraft. After a short while, however, I jumped down from the gunship and drove my tug back to the squadron.

****

Our OV-10s started flying daylight missions in concert with Spectre gunships, now in search of the enemy's big 130mm anti-aircraft guns. Once the target was found, usually by muzzle flashes, the Nail OV-10 or Spectre gunship would "paint" the target with its laser, then call in a Phantom to drop a laser-guided missile on the gun. I had been helping the crew chiefs post-flight their OV-10s and often heard from the air crews of their exploits in conjunction with the Spectres. Even though I was no longer part of the 16th SOS, our missions were directly linked with theirs, and I was constantly being updated as to what was happening. The enemy was on the move in such large numbers, they were no longer able to remain concealed from the air. Our FACs would locate and mark targets for the A-1 Sandys or F-4 Phantoms as well as the AC-130 gunships.

****

We got word of an AC-130 that had landed at Kontum, South Vietnam, to rearm and was subsequently destroyed on the ground by enemy artillery. The crew was okay. Numerous C-130s were damaged or lost due to the intense enemy barrage around Kontum airport. I could feel for their crew chiefs. More and more were losing their charges, both on the ground and in the air. I often wondered about their crews, having served with some of them back at Dyess. I remembered all the practice air-drops we had made on the dirt strip next to the main Dyess runway. This was different of course, because now they were doing it for real and under fire.

****

More of our OV-10s were crash landing at bases in South Vietnam. A few crew chiefs made the short trip to Da Nang Air Base to repair them enough to make it back home to NKP. They would spend a few days patching them up and then crawl into the small cargo compartment behind the pilot's cockpit for the bumpy ride back.

****

One crew chief brought back what he claimed to be a VC skull. It was a human skull all right, but we never knew if it was an enemy's or not. For some time he kept his souvenir proudly on display in his hooch. He loved showing it off and usually carried it everywhere he went. One night as he was passing it around the room, another crew chief grabbed it, stood in the doorway and smashed it down onto the concrete walkway! The VC skull made a sickening sound as it broke into a hundred pieces. The two men almost came to blows but we quickly pulled them apart. The chief said he was tired of looking at the skull and considered it a bad omen. I thought smashing it was itself a bad omen, but I was glad not to have it around anymore.

****

We got word that fellow crew chief John Forsberg's AC-130E, with the 105mm Howitzer, had provided air cover for American personnel under siege at Polei Kleng. The enemy was at the wire with tanks and mortars. By morning, the American commander on the ground reported the situation as "quiet." Later we heard that John's Spectre had been credited with 350 kills and had repulsed a major attack.

****

Our Nail OV-10s were being deployed now every day in search of tanks. In the Central Highlands, one enemy tank had penetrated the outpost's defenses and was actually sitting on top of the Command Bunker in an attempt to crush it. The Nail OV-10 "painted" the tank with its laser, and an Ubon-based F-4 struck the tank, knocking it off the bunker, saving those inside. It was good to know that our efforts were bearing fruit.

Still my attitude towards the war and the North Vietnamese was growing more sinister and aggressive. I casually spoke with a couple of FAC pilots about going up on a mission. They said there were no back seats available, but I could ride in the cargo box if I wanted. The cargo hold at the back of the OV-10 was small, with a hard floor to sit on and no windows. *What would be the point of that?* I thought. Anyway, when they told me about some of their recent "adventures," as one pilot called it, I quickly dropped the idea.

Instead of winding down toward so-called "peace with honor," the war was being waged with more intensity than ever! Our guys were facing bullets and missiles every day. The U.S. Navy and the U.S. Air Force were literally being tasked with saving all of South Vietnam. Think about that.

We worked dawn to dusk and beyond to keep our aircraft airborne. These pilots were among the bravest I'd seen! They would limp back with their aircraft shot full of holes and shortly after, climb back into the cockpit of another Bronco and head back into the fray. We worked seven days a week now, with a single day off only on occasion. We didn't bother keeping track of the days. To us they were all the same. The only way I knew it was Sunday, was when red came up on my Seiko. The war drew a little closer to us now as well. Some of the pilots started reporting light ground fire on approach to the base.

****

Our line chief told us the story one morning of the MIG fly-by. According to the chief, (who was there at the time), one hot sunny day in 1968, a North Vietnamese MIG roared down the NKP runway at fifty feet! It came out of nowhere, under radar, and just as quickly disappeared. He cautioned us to be on the lookout for anything.

****

One OV-10 pilot, upon exiting his aircraft and seeing my Spectre hat, practically bowled me over with handshakes and pats on my back. He had just flown cover for a Spectre gunship. The Special Ops aircraft had maintained a "ring of fire" around fifteen wounded soldiers for several hours, until they were med-evacuated ("medevaced") by U.S. Army helicopters. He couldn't say enough good things about the Spectres. I felt proud.

****

We got word of another Spectre gunship hit by a surface-to-air missile over An Loc. The aircraft made an emergency landing at Tan Son Nhut in South Vietnam. The crew was shaken, but okay. The gunship's crew chief would fly to South Vietnam to start repairs on his bird.

****

I got a tour one afternoon of "Dutch Mill," the super-secret intelligence section located near the flight line. I was shown how the air-dropped sensors along the Ho Chi Minh Trail relayed vital information back to the center at NKP as part of "Operation Igloo White." The information provided us with locations of troops and materiel as they made their way south. This information was relayed to the FACs or gunships. The aircraft then flew to the area and systematically destroyed what they found. I was also shown the area surrounding NKP on a large grid. The technicians pointed out the numerous areas of recent enemy probes at the perimeter. I decided not to wander around the dark streets at night anymore.

****

On June 18, I got a phone call. This was highly unusual. Immediately I thought of home and family, fearing the worst. I left the hangar and went to Squadron Maintenance. It was John Forsberg. What a surprise! But he was calling with bad news. Another Spectre gunship had been shot down. It was No. 043. He thought since I'd been her crew chief for a short while that I should know. "No word on beepers or chutes," he said grimly. John didn't have any more information than that. We talked awhile longer and made plans to somehow get together, but we never did. I had spoken to John for the last time. I raced over to Squadron Operations to see if they had any information about the shoot down. I was struck by the solemn tone in John's voice going over and over in my head. The news, of course, was bad, but even in our brief discussion on other topics he was not his usual self. The war was taking its toll on another good man. I sincerely missed him. Like John Rhett, my friend John Forsberg had a stabilizing effect on me.

Operations said some of our OV-10s and a couple Jolly Greens were on their way to the crash site as we spoke. The air controllers at NKP (call-sign "Invert"), were in communications with "Lion" (Ubon) and "Viking" (Thai-Lao border). They were vectoring the rescue aircraft to the area. The only other information we had was that there were, in fact, some survivors. I went back to my hangar but I couldn't concentrate. The maintenance chief, now "Mr. Mellow," said I should grab a tug and head over to the Knife squadron of Jolly Greens. He said if they pick anyone up, they'll drop them here on the flight line. I commandeered a tug and bounced down the flight line to the helicopter squadron and waited.

Sometime later, the Jolly Greens came into view. When they touched down, I drove my tug over to the choppers. As usual, a crowd started to form around the Jolly Greens. The side door slid open and out came Sgt. Patterson! The last time I saw him was at the Spectre snack bar two months earlier. Here he was, stepping down out of the rescue helicopter. Someone handed him a beer. He looked weary.

"Combs, is that you?" he asked, as people gathered around him. He was shaking everyone's hands and receiving numerous pats on his back. "It's damn good to see you!" I asked him what happened, and he took a long deep breath and began his story.

They were flying southwest of Hue, in South Vietnam, he said, in search of targets. He was flying as rear scanner, and noted a flash of light that arced its way up toward the gunship. As it approached, he got up and prepared to launch a flare to divert the missile away from the aircraft. He fired off a flare but the missile continued right in and hit them in the right wing. The No. 3 engine exploded and fell off the aircraft. The engineer said on interphone that they were losing altitude. Someone made a mayday call. Just as he started to buckle on his parachute, the right wing came off, sending them down in a spiral. Some of the gunners were pinned to the side of the fuselage by the centrifugal force, with their arms outstretched, as if to say "help me!" Patterson was blown out the cargo door by fresh explosions and struggled to fasten his chute harness as he fell through the night sky. The flight engineer and one other crew member were able to bail out through the forward scanner's opening. Of the fifteen on board, only three managed to escape. He said he lay quietly in the bushes until the morning when the FACs started circling overhead. To his relief they rescued him, without incident, from the jungle.

I shook his hand as the medics hustled him away. The other two crewmen were put into an ambulance and driven away. I never saw Patterson again after that day on the flight line. His story made me sick to my stomach. I began to think about some of the gunners I knew in his crew and of the gunship I had worked so hard to keep flying. Now they were gone! In a daze, I drove the tug back to the hangar and without turning off the engine, sat there and cried. The maintenance chief came over and, as he switched off the motor, told me to go back to my hooch. History shows that Spectre gunship tail number 043 was the first AC-130 shot down over South Vietnam.

That night, Sparky, Fred, Dan and I went to a party at the Officers' Club. We had been invited by some of the OV-10 pilots. I smoked a joint before going. It didn't help. When we got there, a live band was just starting to play. They had some Taiwanese dancing girls on stage. I got drunk. That didn't help either. Back at our hooch after the party, I got undressed and went to bed. Probably because of how much liquor I had consumed, the room immediately began to swirl around me. I fell asleep or passed out, I'm not sure which. In any case, I found myself experiencing for the first time, a horrible nightmare.

In the "dream"...*I was in my gunship kneeling near the forward scanner's position trying to open my tool box. The red combat lighting made it difficult to see the lock. We were airborne but in a steep dive. I could see outside past the right-side scanner. Bright white sparks were flying violently off number three engine. We had been hit! Someone made a mayday call over the radio as I struggled to open my tool box. The AC-130 started to make a right wing roll-over. Spent shells and loose equipment were flying all around. I was hit numerous times by flying debris. It seemed everyone was screaming over the radio at once. Despite our rollover, I was finally able to open my tool box just as another explosion rocked the aircraft. The noise was deafening. What tool do I need? I felt a strange jolt and vibration and saw more bright flashes in the night sky. We had been hit again. What tool fixes this? Some crewmembers were scrambling past, heading toward the back of the aircraft and the long row of parachutes. Because the gunship was in a spinning dive, the crew kept bouncing off the sides of the aircraft as they tried to make their way to safety. I had to hold on to the scanner seat legs to stay near my tool box. I kept rummaging through the large metal box and all its compartments, looking for some elusive tool. We were being tossed about abruptly in all directions. The copilot jumped down from the flight deck and raced to my side screaming, "FIX IT CHIEF, FIX IT!" His face became a splash of red as shells tore through the fuselage and into his upper body. By instinct I turned away to face the right scanner who was now covered in blood as well. Constant hammering on the left side of the aircraft was suddenly replaced by another loud explosion. I noticed flames erupting near the 20mm guns, and I could smell the distinct odor of jet fuel. I looked down at my legs and saw blood. As I wiped my forehead with my sleeve, it came away bloody. I was soaked in dark crimson blood, visible even in this red light. I didn't know if it was mine or someone else's; it didn't seem to matter. The scanner reached down with his left hand to help me stand up. We locked eyes for a brief moment. I grabbed his hand with both of mine. Just then the right wing came off, plunging us into a cart-wheeling dive. Another bright flash followed by a loud explosion...and I woke up.*

I was drenched all right, but in sweat rather than blood. I jumped from my bunk to the floor. Fred was awake and asked if I was okay. "Yeah, I think so," I muttered. It took a few moments to clear my head. I was elated to discover that it had only been a nightmare, and I was safe on the ground. Fred got up and we both dressed and headed to the chow hall for some fresh air and hot coffee. I related my experience in detail to Fred, once I had stopped shaking. After some hot coffee, encouraging words from a friend and a cold shower back at the hooch area, I went back to bed.

The following day was a rare scheduled day off for me. I went to the base chaplain. He told me my boots were dirty and that I needed a haircut. Thanks for nothing!

I started smoking more and caring less. There seemed to be just no end to the cycle of death and destruction. For added misery, the monsoons managed to keep us wet most of the time as well. The line chief came by our hangar one day and asked me if I wanted to test for staff sergeant. I said no. He insisted and said at least we would be dry in the testing office, and it would consume most of a day. I relented and said okay. Two days later, a few of us from the flight line took our tests. We stayed cool and dry all day.

****

Practically every day, a giant C-141 transport landed and took off again. It delivered new troops just starting their tours. It also took home the troops who had completed their one-year tours. We called it the "Freedom Bird."

I was starting to get short. I had just under one hundred days left in-country. I was a "two-digit midget." I started a short-timer's calendar, which I tacked to the wall beside my bunk. The gecko lizards that lived in our room paid no attention to my calendar. We called them "fuck-you" lizards. This was because of their high-pitched squeal, which sounded as if they were saying, "fuck you." They were a common sight around our rooms, usually with a few occupying the wall at any given time. One morning as I was climbing out of bed, I grabbed the post and immediately felt a large squishy lizard body under my hand! It reacted by trying to bite me, but I threw it off, sending it crashing against the opposite wall. Fuck you, lizard!

One afternoon we watched from the flight line as the Freedom Bird lifted off the NKP runway with most of us wishing we were on it and heading back to the world. At the end of the runway, the C-141 was still struggling to get airborne. It barely passed over the tree-tops and then dropped down out of sight. We all waited and held our breaths expecting the explosion and fire that was sure to come. Seconds later, it reappeared and climbed away from the steaming jungle. We thought how ironic that would be for us to complete our tours, only to crash on the way home!

Most of us agreed, we would want to preflight the Freedom Bird ourselves before we got on it.

****

One day, a group of us filled out our "dream sheets" for our next assignment. The Air Force would "try" to place us near an area we desired. It usually didn't happen that way, however. At first I thought about listing bases on the East Coast, figuring that by Air Force logic, I would end up on the West Coast. In the end, I listed my top ten locations—all along the West Coast.

I was by now carrying a chip on my shoulder and pushing the limits on regulations. I grew my hair and mustache beyond the regular standards. I wore colorful beads around my neck. I was becoming a "military hippie." I was not alone, of course, as morale in the military, particularly in Southeast Asia, was at an all-time low. Racial tensions were high at this time as well. For the most part the blacks stayed together and ate together. They went through a long and drawn out handshake every time another one entered the room. Of course we were excluded from the ritual. Some of our crew chiefs were black, and we worked side by side on the flight line. Some were friends of mine. But after work as we walked into the chow hall together, our friends would abruptly move off to be with their brothers. It was awkward and sometimes openly hostile. I just did my job and stayed close to the hooch area.

I continued to pencil out the days on my short-timer's calendar. My one-year tour was ending. I never did take an R&R, and at the most had an occasional day off only here and there. I was tired both physically and emotionally.

A few new guys arrived from the States to start their year-long tours. Most of them wanted to know what it was like and what they should expect. I gave them my perspective, for what it was worth.

****

The rainy season was winding down as we approached October 1972. The war was raging and we were constantly repairing new battle damage to our OV-10s. President Nixon was on the verge of being reelected back in the world. He secretly ordered the resumption of the bombing up north. The Jolly Greens were being sent out on search and rescue missions almost every day now. Unfortunately, more American aircraft were being shot down as well.

A few weeks before I was scheduled to rotate back to the World, I got my orders for my new duty station. I was to go to the 41st Aerospace

Rescue and Recovery Squadron at Hamilton AFB in San Francisco, California. I would be working on HC-130H aircraft. I mentioned my next assignment to one of our pilots the next day and he smiled and replied, "You'll love it there. It's beautiful and close to the ocean." The young pilot turned his head for a moment then looking down the NKP flight line said, "It's a great place, I wish I were going there myself... good luck." He shook my hand as we walked toward his OV-10 parked on the ramp.

The new assignment was a lift to my spirits. I yearned to be back on C-130s again, and California would be a short distance from home in Washington State. I would be going alone as everyone else I knew was getting orders for bases all over the U.S. Our goodbyes would be final.

I had written home to Denise about our new assignment. She arranged to meet me at the airport in San Francisco. We would then drive together north to Hamilton AFB to check it out. Hopefully, we would find a place to live, on the base if possible. I was concerned that little Tracy would not recognize me and that I had changed so much that my family would worry over me.

I had a minor altercation with the sergeant in charge of the tool crib (here we go again). He was going to prevent my rotation home unless I found a missing socket or something. I told him to take his socket and shove it! Sparky ran to the flight line and grabbed the tool from his tool box and came back, pressing it into my palm. I stuck my hand in my pocket and pulled it out again with a grin and said, "Is this what you're looking for?" I tossed it at the sergeant and stormed out of his office. I was fed up with some personnel who only cared about their rules and regulations. Didn't he realize people were fighting and dying all around us? No, he just wanted his precious socket. I was totally burned out!

****

I helped launch and recover our OV-10s on the flight line for a couple of days, before it was my turn to jump onboard the Freedom Bird.

One afternoon, I was in the forward cockpit of an OV-10 when my sleeve caught the ejection handle. As I moved, I felt a tug on my arm from the resistance. My heart stopped! Luckily, I had not switched on power to the aircraft and would not have been ejected anyway, but it shook me just the same.

Finally, the last day arrived and a group of my friends, including Sparky, Fred and Dan, escorted me to the departure gate for my trip home. We took some pictures, shook hands, promised to write, and soon I was walking alone up the stairs into the C-141. I sat down on a blue seat facing aft and strapped in. As the giant transport lifted off the NKP runway, the interior of the aircraft erupted with shouts and hollers and applause. I remained silent. I was glad to be going home for sure, but I was also leaving good friends behind. I thought about my two gunships and their crews. They would not be coming home. Somehow, it wasn't fair that I was.

ELEVEN

Hamilton Air Force Base

OUR C-141 FLEW HIGH ACROSS LAOS AND SOUTH VIETNAM on its way to Clark Air Base in the Philippines. It was dark when we touched down at Clark field. I checked in to the transient barracks for the night. We were to grab a commercial flight from there to Travis AFB in California. Our flight would leave early the next morning.

I had dinner at the NCO club and then wandered around the base for a while. The Philippines had suffered from major floods only a month or two before. I noticed the 405th fighter wing had pitched in with the locals to clean up the damage. That was the Air Force way.

While roaming around the base, I was amazed to see families—men, women and children—watching a baseball game on a beautiful green field. The smell of freshly cut grass, the crack of the bat, along with the cheers of the crowd swept over me. I watched for a while, just breathing in this atmosphere of normalcy. I realized that while I was part of the war machine, normal everyday life was still going on. I wanted to jump up and scream at the people, "Don't you realize Americans are fighting and dying and crashing, while you laugh and play?" I didn't, of course, but it made me sad that no one seemed to care or notice. I went back to the barracks and slept. I dozed off, wondering if I would ever feel "normal" again.

The next morning, I boarded a commercial jet for the flight home. Wow! American stewardesses greeted each of us as we entered the airplane. They were beautiful! And our first taste of home.

As we lifted off the runway, shouts of joy filled the compartment. I kept quiet and looked out the window. Our airliner quickly rose into the morning sun, slipping through layers of clouds. I realized with each passing moment that I was leaving death behind me, as rapidly as I was closing in on the safety of home. The World was far off still…but getting closer. I slept most of the way across the Pacific.

After a long flight, we finally touched down at Travis AFB, just outside San Francisco. Some guys kissed the ground when they got off the plane. I went into the terminal's restroom to change out of my uniform. We knew already that to be seen in a military uniform was to invite being spit upon. Welcome home! Once in civilian clothes, I grabbed a taxi with a couple of other guys, and we rode along the freeway to San Francisco Airport. I was amazed at how fast everyone was going!

We were soon pulling up to the main terminal at the airport. I was nervous as I approached the area where I was to meet Denise. After a short time searching among the faces in the crowd, I found her. She was beautiful! She was wearing a mini-skirt and her hair was longer than I remembered. We hugged and kissed for a long time. It felt so good to be in her arms. We walked hand in hand to the car rental counter. After the arrangements were completed, we were given the keys to a car and directions to find it. As we walked to the parking lot I couldn't take my eyes off my wife. She was captivating.

Denise offered to sit behind the wheel, and since I hadn't driven anything but a flight line tug in a year, I agreed. Again the sheer pace of freeway traffic was a shock. Everything seemed to be whirling around me. We headed north toward Hamilton AFB. Along the way, we stopped at a motel for the night. I spent most of the night in the bathroom, throwing up. I was very nervous. This night just did not seem real. For the past year I had thought endlessly about this particular night… my first night home safe in the arms of my wife. Now it all seemed like a dream.

The next morning, we continued north to Hamilton AFB. Denise continued to drive as I was still unprepared for the fast pace around me. When we arrived at Hamilton, we found an available apartment located on the base. We arranged to move in. I was on a one-month leave, so we would return in approximately three weeks. Denise drove us back to the airport in San Francisco, after a brief tour around Hamilton AFB. Just as the OV-10 pilot had said, it was beautiful there. We caught a flight to Seattle and before long were in the air heading home.

My family met us at Sea-Tac Airport. Little Tracy was there and would have nothing to do with me. It hurt my feelings, but I had expected it and knew she would warm up to her daddy with time.

We spent a couple of weeks at home, just trying to relax and have fun. I was cold in the 60-degree temperature and wore a heavy coat most of the time. I was glad to see that all my stereo gear had arrived safely, thanks to John Forsberg.

We went to a few parties with old friends, but I didn't feel as if we had much in common anymore. I found myself drifting back to the Spectre revetments at Ubon. I kept seeing the faces of my crews as they prepared for flight or had returned from a combat mission. The crews on board 044 and 043 were officially listed as missing-in-action (MIA). Were they chained to a cage somewhere in the jungles of Laos? Or were they dead? I didn't share my sorrow with my friends or family. They were happy to see me home and I didn't want to bring them down. I tried to put on a happy face.

Before long, it was time to pack up for the drive south to Hamilton Air Force Base. Cousin Gerry had taken my Corvette off blocks and had it ready to go. It looked great! My brothers and my cousin had made sure it was well taken care of the year I was gone. Gerry had been given a medical discharge from the Army after it was discovered he had cancer. He looked great, though, and said it was in remission, which forced me to stop worrying about him. At least he wasn't jumping out of airplanes anymore. Still, I was very proud of him for serving and fighting the battle for his life.

We decided Denise and Tracy would drive the VW down to California. Bob, a friend of the family, would assist us in the drive south. I noticed how Bob, Denise and Tracy seemed to act like a close-knit family. Tracy would run to Bob, but still avoid me. I felt as if I had been replaced.

The drive to California was uneventful. Although driving the Corvette was as exhilarating as I'd remembered it. I had wired up a stereo headphone jack into a hidden spot in the console, so I enjoyed sounds like never before while buzzing along at speed. We "caravanned," so I couldn't just leave my family in the dust, but I would lag behind on occasion so that I'd have to speed up to reach them. Driving with headphones on is risky and illegal, but I just didn't care.

Soon we were unpacking at our little apartment on base. After a few days, we took Bob to the airport for his flight back to Seattle. We were finally alone and a family once more.

I processed into the 41st Air Rescue and Recovery Squadron and reported to the commander for duty. I was provided a tour of the flight line and a rundown on the squadron's mission. We had twelve of the new H model C-130s. These HC-130s were painted a light gray color with "Rescue" painted across the vertical stabilizer. Black letters spelling out U.S. Air Force were on both sides of the fuselage. There was a large white radome on top of the fuselage, just forward of the wings. The nose was squared off and held the aluminum recovery forks of the Fulton Recovery System. This was the same system used on the MC-130 Combat Talon aircraft. Long fiberglass lines ran from the nose to the tips of each wing. The system used a helium balloon on the end of a 500 ft. line. Whatever was to be retrieved was attached to the end of the long line. The HC-130 would approach at slow speed (around 150 mph), lock the line between the forks and reel in the load with a winch through the open cargo door.

The long lines to the wing tips prevented the recovery line from fouling the props in case of a miss. Two large square Plexiglas windows had been added to each side of the forward fuselage. The primary mission of the squadron was to retrieve downed space capsules, weather reconnaissance and coastal search and rescue.

I was assigned to an aircraft as crew chief. My new charge was aircraft No. 69-5830. Once again, I was back in my element. I set about becoming familiarized with my new airplane. As always, the crew chief has ultimate authority of the aircraft on the ground. It was I who would decide if the aircraft was fit to fly. I went through the aircraft log-book to assess its history. The sergeant who had been the crew chief was transferred to another base. I spent a few days just going over all the systems of the aircraft. The first full day I conducted inspections and repaired or replaced any components in need. Within the first week, I felt familiar enough with my aircraft to answer any questions the flight crew might have. It felt good to be back on a C-130 again. It was comforting to know that trip flares would not be going off at night around the perimeter. I also would not have to worry about snipers at night anymore. Still, I could not get my two gunships out of my mind. Being around a C-130 of course was a constant reminder, but I would not have had it any other way.

I was the only crew chief among those in the squadron with gunship experience and most of the others wanted to know what it was like. I kept my sorrow to myself and usually only talked about the technical side of "owning" a gunship. A number of other guys told me they wished for a chance to be a Spectre Crew Chief.

The Christmas holidays were almost upon us. Little Tracy was slowly warming up to her daddy. Denise and I bought her a rocking horse for Christmas. Every time we would see an animal larger than a dog from the windows of the car, Tracy would point and squeal "horsey!"

We made the drive south to Disneyland one weekend, and Tracy was overwhelmed! Her favorite activity was, of course, the western horseback ride. They were actually mules, but not to Tracy. She went on the ride three times. We had to pry her off of the animal! This was the beginning of a lifelong affection for darling Tracy; I love that about her. We had a fun-filled day and I was feeling rejuvenated by the atmosphere that is unique to Disneyland. Tracy had her picture taken with the life-size Mickey Mouse. She didn't look too happy about it, though.

As we were leaving the park, walking toward the main gate, I rounded the corner on Main Street and faced Jiminy Cricket. The person inside the costume didn't speak, but he waved to us and reached for Tracy's hand as we brushed by. I felt a cold flush come over me as I flashed to the 23rd OV-10s parked on the flight line. "Good job, Jiminy!" I yelled to the character as he walked away with a wave. He had no idea why I said that, or what I really meant. His world was about as far removed from war as could be. I felt envious of whoever was in that cricket suit. This was all so unreal!

****

A few of the guys at NKP continued to write letters. I received a letter from Sparky detailing a search and rescue operation over a downed AC-130. The aircraft was "Thor" No. 490. There were no survivors. *Merry Christmas!*

I also received a letter from John Forsberg. He was soon to be rotating back to the States. He said sergeants Fenter, Reaid and Fuller were among the crew lost with No. 490. More friends killed in a meaningless conflict. It put a damper on my holidays, but I tried not to show it. John sounded different in his letter. He was being sent to a base on the East Coast, and by his comments I could tell the war had definitely taken a toll on him, as well.

January 1973 brought a cease-fire in Vietnam. The Air Force established a new headquarters at NKP under General Vogt. The remote base I had left behind now exercised control over all air operations for S.E. Asia.

I got word that my promotion to staff sergeant had come through. It meant a few dollars more a month, which we could certainly use. Now I was glad that I had taken the time to get out of the sweltering heat just to take the test months before. Denise insisted we go down to the BX and buy the new stripes. I proudly sewed on the blue and silver staff sergeant stripes and ironed my best fatigues. Yeah, it felt good.

****

My aircraft usually flew training missions off the California coast. We trained in search and rescue techniques, as well as space capsule recovery. We practiced snaring weather balloons with the Fulton recovery system. It was amazing to watch the process from this vantage point, and it felt good to be flying in my own one-thirty again.

Often during pre-flights I found myself walking around the non-existent 20mm guns. I was still used to avoiding the myriad of equipment on the AC-130s. My new aircraft had a relatively wide open cargo area and of course, no booth.

During coastal flights my HC-130 would approach storms rather than avoid them like most flyers are expected to do. On one flight heading into a storm, we felt and heard a loud bang. I was in the flight deck at the time and instinctively looked at the engine gauges. Everything appeared normal. The navigator said some of his direction finding equipment was acting strange. Once we landed back at Hamilton, I got on top of the aircraft and discovered that we had been hit by lightning. I performed a post-flight inspection of the aircraft and wrote up the torched antenna for replacement.

The work schedule at Hamilton was much less grueling than Southeast Asia. I actually had weekends off! Denise and I made friends easily with some of our neighbors and on weekends, we would drive down to San Francisco or out to the ocean beaches. I particularly enjoyed the ocean with its majestic beauty and calming surf. I was beginning to find myself again. I discovered that being around children had a very relaxing effect on me. They were so joyful and full of innocence. I longed for some of those qualities to rekindle my spirit. I enjoyed watching little Tracy playing in the sand and frolicking in the waves as they tickled her feet.

On one trip to the ocean, we stumbled upon a nude beach. We walked its length and back again. I felt conspicuous in my swimsuit but kept it on. I did of course, enjoy the sights of the young California girls who were less inhibited than I was.

The first two months of 1973 rolled by. The squadron's training missions were scaled back and our aircraft flew less and less each month. March brought Operation Homecoming to Travis AFB. The American POWs were returning to the United States after being held prisoners in Hanoi. Travis was a short distance away, so I thought about going. But, I also knew that no prisoners from Laos had been released. I watched it unfold on TV like most Americans. I knew all along, however, that more remained behind. Still, I watched closely, looking and hoping for a familiar face. I saw none.

Mom flew down from Seattle to pay us a visit and pay she did. Little

Tracy was at this time discovering the wonders of the flushing toilet. We have no proof, but it appears that most of Mom's travel money saw action with Tracy. I was mortified. Mom, as only my mom can be, took it all in stride. After all, she did raise four boys the likes of me! She reminded me of the various things we as children had lost or broken. Mom, I will always love you!

I was proud to show my mother the flight line and my aircraft parked nearby. I couldn't take her onboard, but did get close enough to show her my name stenciled on the side of the C-130. I could see the pride in her eyes and that raised my spirits. Time passed quickly and soon we said goodbye at the airport. I was sorry to see her go, but I knew it was only a short time until we would be coming home, as well.

****

I maintained a perfect record on aborts; I had zero. At no time that I was in charge of an aircraft, did that aircraft return or fail to take off due to mechanical issues. It would not be a major problem of course on training flights, as the mission could simply be rescheduled. I took great pride in the fact that while sending my aircraft into combat, never once did it return, having failed to fly its mission due to mechanical difficulties. In combat the difference was life or death, saving lives or taking them. It was all a matter of perspective. I could claim, as my four years were drawing to a close, that I never failed in my duty. If I found my plane to be too dangerous to fly, I grounded it. As crew chief I had final authority to make that decision. I did not take that responsibility lightly.

****

One morning, I was sipping coffee in the flight deck. I was working on my aircraft records when a colonel stomped up the stairs. He demanded we get engines running and get in the air right away! As I turned to look at who was making these demands, I noticed this colonel was not wearing a security badge or a name tag. I stood up from the navigator's table and told the officer, "Sir, with respect…get the hell off my aircraft before I throw you off." As I moved towards him, he backed down the stairs and out the crew door. Before I could get down the stairs and outside myself, he was walking briskly towards the maintenance shack. I re-entered my aircraft and went back to work, knowing I had not heard the end of this. I was prepared to defend my position, but I didn't have to. A short while later I noticed the line chief and a few others walking my way. The colonel was with them. I met them at the crew entrance door, effectively blocking their entrance. The chief spoke first, explaining to me that I had just passed a security test and should be proud. The colonel also said I did the right thing and offered me his hand.

"No hard feelings, Colonel?" I asked.

"None whatsoever, Sergeant," he replied.

"Good job!"

"Thank you, sir." I said.

Later that morning, I heard another C-130 starting engines, and I knew the colonel, (who was really a major) had found his mark. We had security briefings for a week after that, and I was used as one example of how to do it right. I didn't tell anybody that I had failed that same test a few lifetimes ago.

****

The young technical sergeant that ran the squadron tool crib had a big problem. He was married with a six-year-old daughter who had terminal cancer. He needed time off to be with his family. The maintenance chief asked me to fill in for him while he was away. Imagine that, me in charge of the tool crib! I did double duty for a while, maintaining my aircraft and watching over the tool section. It was in a shambles. It was obvious that this sergeant didn't have his mind on his job—and for good reason. I took the time to get his shop reorganized. About three weeks later, he returned to the squadron. He was amazed when he stepped inside his now rearranged office. I asked him how his daughter was. "She died," he said. I told him how sorry I was. He explained that on their final trip to the hospital in San Francisco, his daughter said matter-of-factly, "I'm not coming home again, am I?" She had known and faced her own death with dignity. She had expressed her love for Mommy and Daddy and told them she would always be with them. All this from a six-year-old girl! I cried openly as he told me his story. I realized that day that I had been feeling sorry for myself, for the loss of my crews, my two aircraft and my friends. If a six-year-old girl could be that strong, then so should I. That poor sergeant didn't realize that in his grief over the loss of his daughter, he helped to heal the deep melancholy inside me. I hugged my little Tracy longer and tighter that night and thanked God for my family.

****

Denise, Tracy and I were paid a surprise visit by my younger brother, Maurie, and his friend, Rod. They stayed around for a few days and enjoyed the California sun. We scrounged some plywood from the squadron supply shop and built a very sturdy cabinet to house my elaborate stereo set-up. It was great in California, but my brother's visit made me homesick. Shortly after Maurie left, we got a surprise visit from my Air Force buddy, Bob Ittes. He was stationed at Vandenberg AFB, located in Southern California. Over a few drinks he filled me in on the last couple of years. Bob had spent 1970-71 in Vietnam. He was working on O-2 birddog FACs at Tan Son Nhut as crew chief for about six months, before being re-assigned to Cam Ranh Bay. At Cam Ranh, Bob had been a crew chief on C-123Ks. I was stunned to discover that his aircraft and crew were lost when his plane was shot down. We had been years and miles apart, yet suffered similar ordeals. Bob was equally surprised to hear about the shoot-down of my gunship. What really surprised me though, was the news that he had re-enlisted! I would be getting out in a few months, but my buddy Bob was now faced with a few more years. Of course I teased him about it. As Bob shook hands before roaring away in his yellow Porsche, I knew it would be years before we would see each other again. Being with him only for a couple of days, revitalized me, and for that I was grateful.

****

As I prepared my aircraft one day for another training mission, the crew van pulled up and the flight crew jumped out. As I did my walk-around with the pilot, I noticed a familiar face in his crew. The navigator had flown with Spectre during my tour with the Air Commandos. He recognized me about the same time. We shook hands and he patted me on the back. "You were Zero Four Four weren't you?" he asked.

"Yes sir, I was." I answered.

"I flew with Rams a number of times," he said. "He was one of the best." I agreed. "Ubon was attacked again in October," he continued. "They shot two of them in the barbed wire, just behind the Spec revetments."

I told him a little about my early-out move to NKP and the 23rd Nail OV-10s. He had good things to say about the Nail Broncos as we walked up the steps of my airplane. I sat on the lower crew bunk, next to the navigator's table. The young captain and I reminisced about some of the good times and bad times we shared with the Air Commandos of the 16th SOS. I had mentioned something about having come from Dyess AFB when the pilot came up the stairs to the flight deck. "Good old Dyess AFB in Abilene, Texas," the pilot said. He had been there with the 348th, about the same time I was there in the 347th. *It's a small world,* I thought to myself as the three of us sat in the flight deck swapping stories.

We flew a local mission that day and landed back at Hamilton a few hours later. I didn't know it at the time, but I had just flown my last C-130 mission. Looking back now, it was fitting that the crew had ties to Dyess and Ubon.

****

We got word that the squadron was moving to McClellan AFB outside Sacramento. It would take a couple of months to complete the move. I only had two months left in my four-year enlistment. I would not be going with them unless I re- enlisted.

I had been counseled about the great prospects of another four-year term in the Air Force and would receive a sizable bonus if I did re-up. I did some soul searching and discussed it with Denise, and we both agreed that four years had been enough. I was promised another stripe and I could train to be a flight engineer if I stayed in, but I could also expect to be away from my family a great deal. I wanted to settle down and go back to college for my degree. It was settled. When the squadron moved, I would stay behind.

Word got around the squadron that I was a short-timer and would not be going north with the rest of them. One afternoon, I was summoned to the line chief 's office. As I stood in front of his desk, three of my fellow crew chiefs grabbed me from behind. They lifted me into the air and carried me out of the office. We went down the hall and into the latrine. Once inside, one of them turned on the cold water in the shower and I was forced in, clothes and all. They all laughed as I struggled to no avail. It was the familiar ritual bestowed upon air and ground crew members who were leaving. I was shocked and surprised, but enjoyed every minute of it. I thought of Capt. Halpin's splash down after what was supposed to be his last combat flight on gunships.

****

As the squadron aircraft departed on their one-way trips to McClellan, I asked the scheduling office to hold back my aircraft until the last group was to leave. Day by day, the flight line grew lonelier and quieter as our HC-130s flew out loaded with squadron gear to Sacramento. As each aircraft departed, I said goodbye to my friends and colleagues. As they started up engines, I helped pull the chocks or marshal the aircraft and crew to the taxi-way.

Back in our little apartment, life was slowly returning to normal. I still thought about death every day though and couldn't get myself to relax. I remember watching "The Tonight Show" starring Johnny Carson and not being able to laugh and enjoy the fun. I used to love that show! Now, I wondered how and why people wasted their time with frivolity and corny jokes while American troops were still dying. I knew I had to break out of this…but how?

****

My aircraft had developed a fuel leak in No.1 engine, and I spent a day or two working on a solution. It was night on the flight line, and we were running the engine to be sure I had solved the problem. As I stood before my aircraft with headphones on, I conferred with the maintenance chief in the flight deck. No, I did not see fuel dripping anymore, I told him. "Closer," he said, "get closer." I moved slowly towards the spinning prop of number one engine and still saw no evidence of fuel. Before I knew it, I was less than five feet away from the four-bladed props as they roared in front of me. We had been taught not to watch the spinning props as they could have a hypnotizing effect.

It was true that in the past, more than one crew chief had been killed by accidentally walking into the giant spinning props. For a fleeting second, I could see how easy it would be to become disoriented by the sight and sound of the jet engine and its blurred propellers. Knowing this, I still found myself inching forward closer still, closer than I had ever stood before. At their lowest arc the props could cut across my neck and chest. A couple more feet and I would be decapitated. I knew this in my mind, but I still inched closer. "Okay, Sarge, I'm shutting her down," boomed suddenly in my headphones. The chief 's voice snapped me back from the trance I was in. My concentration broken, I backed away from the still rotating props and headed towards the crew entrance door. The engine checked out fine.

I started to shiver. Was I just cold or did I realize how close I had come? I remembered a couple of years back, John Forsberg had told me how he had pulled the chocks on his aircraft one day and threw them in the crew entrance door. This means nothing until you realize the crew entrance door is in *front* of the props. Usually we would jump down from the left or right paratroop door, pull the chocks from the main wheel well and toss them back inside the paratroop door, all the while staying safely behind the props. John had realized, only after they were airborne, that to put the chocks in the crew entrance door, he would have had to walk between the spinning prop and the side of the aircraft. This was an area about as wide as his shoulders!

****

Hamilton AFB was having an open house and my aircraft was selected for public static display. I already had it in good working order, so now

I simply cleaned everything and got it prepared for show. For the last time, I re-stenciled my name above the crew entrance door as the aircraft's crew chief. We towed the 130 up the flight line to the central staging area. Other aircraft on display would be from the other units on base. There was a HC-135 from the weather reconnaissance squadron, a HH-53 helicopter, A T-37 two-seat trainer and an F-106 Delta Dart from the fighter squadron.

For the next three days, I proudly showed off my aircraft to the military and civilian families that visited the flight line. I conducted tours through the cargo compartment and even allowed some children to sit in the pilot's seat in the flight deck. I felt as if things were coming around full circle as I explained the aircraft's systems to youngsters who might someday be Air Force crew chiefs themselves.

****

Sparky was rotating home from NKP and would be able to spend a day or two with me before going on home to Indiana. He had been writing letters to keep me informed about the progress of the war and what some of our friends had been doing. In his last letter he told me about a B-52 that crashed short of the NKP runway. Most in the crew bailed out just before it went down. It had taken hits over Hanoi and was limping back home, when they tried to divert to NKP. They almost made it. I could tell Sparky had gotten his fill of the war and was ready to come home.

Denise and I drove over to Travis AFB on the appointed day and brought Sparky back to our house. It was great to see an old friend again, but I did notice that he was not his usual jovial self. More pilots had been lost and OV-10s shot down. Sparky looked tense and worried. I tried to put him at ease as best I could. We spent a day at the ocean and some time down at the flight line. All too soon, he had to leave for home. We took him to the airport in San Francisco and said goodbye. I never heard from him again after that. Sparky my old friend, I do miss you.

****

The flight line was fast becoming a ghost town as most of the assigned aircraft had made the move north. One of the pilots from the F-106 squadron invited me for a ride in his jet. We talked about it, but it never happened. He and his F-106 flew up to McClellan.

My last day on the flight line arrived and I spent most of the time loading my aircraft for its move. I wrote a short note in the log book for the next crew chief. I made sure all write-ups had been cleared so that he could inherit a nearly perfect aircraft. Before the flight crew came out, I had time alone with my airplane and spent long minutes in each area as I did my last preflight. I remembered back to the early days at Dyess and wondered where my first aircraft, No. 805 was. I thought about No. 044 and No. 043, of course, and wondered about the fate of their crews. They were still listed as MIAs. Now, sitting in the flight deck of No. 830 for the last time, I realized it was all coming to an end.

It wasn't long after that the crew van pulled up and I did my last walk-around with the pilot. Now on the interphone and standing in front of the aircraft, I cleared my throat and began engine start-up procedures.

"Ready to start three?" asked the young pilot.

"Three is clear," I said.

"Starting three" he responded.

We went through the procedure for all four engines. Before long, I had pulled the power unit away and, before disconnecting the interphone, asked the flight crew to take good care of my airplane. I heard the pilot, copilot, navigator, flight engineer and even the assistant crew chief, come on the line to say goodbye and good luck.

Once disconnected, I stood in front of the giant aircraft and for the last time, executed a crisp salute and thumbs-up to the pilot. However, the pilot wasn't the only one to return my salute, as the whole crew gave me salutes and thumbs-up in unison. It was a good thing I had my sunglasses on, as tears were streaming down both cheeks. With arms outstretched, I marshaled the aircraft to my right and onto the taxi-way. I stood on the now empty flight line and watched the C-130 taxi to the end of the runway. A few minutes later my airplane rumbled past as it lifted from the runway. I saw for the last time as it roared by "SSgt. Combs, Crew Chief " reflecting off the sun just above the crew entrance door. To my surprise, the aircraft circled once and dipped its wings before disappearing into the twilight.

Epilogue

ITHIN DAYS OF THE SQUADRON'S DEPARTURE, we had our furniture shipped to Washington and finally stood on the lawn saying goodbye to our neighbors. Two days after leaving Hamilton AFB I was home in Bellevue, Washington, facing an uneasy future. The first year I landed a few odd jobs, but found no satisfaction in them. I was used to responsibilities not found in the civilian sector at my level. After "owning" a multi-million dollar aircraft, driving a delivery truck around town brought no joy nor reward. We talked about re-enlistment, but for me, that was a last option. I needed to settle down and begin a career. We struggled, but eventually Denise and I were able to buy our own home and we had another child. Jesse Thomas Combs was born August 10, 1975.

The G.I. Bill would cover a college education, so I chose to go back to school. I earned an Associate's Degree in Early Childhood Education from Bellevue College. Upon graduation, I enrolled at The University Of Washington where I earned a Bachelor's Degree in Social Psychology. Even with the college degrees, good paying jobs were hard to find. This took a toll on our marriage. I will accept the blame. I was not a good husband and we fought all the time; usually over money. I separated from Denise in 1979. Our divorce was finalized about a year later. I put my strongest efforts into being a good father to Tracy and Jesse.

Eventually I met and fell in love with my current wife, Ruth. She had just gone through a divorce as well. I did my best to be a father to her two young boys. Her oldest son, Shean, lived with his father about 100 miles away in Eastern Washington. We cared for her young son, Jason, living with us. Life was not always easy with my new extended family but we made the most of it. Love carried us through.

I have been blessed with beautiful children and now grandchildren as well. Tracy has three wonderful boys: Tristan, Tanner and Ryder. Jesse and his wife, Alyse, have two darling children, Addison and Alexander. I hope someday when they are grown my story will be of value to them. I love my family! Denise passed away from Alzheimer's disease in November 2015. May God rest her soul.

I am so fortunate to have the love of my wife Ruth, my children and my entire family to sustain me. We are now semi-retired and living on a small island in Washington. I continue to practice karate and play drums in a rock and roll band. It keeps me busy.

As of 2017, the Lockheed C-130 aircraft is still being produced at the giant manufacturing plant in Georgia. The C-130 has been used in an ever-expanding role and has probably seen a greater variety of configurations than any other aircraft in modern history. The gunship versions are now under the new Special Operations Command and based in Florida. The new AC-130J model has in-flight refueling capabilities, heads-up displays for the pilot and copilot, better avionics and larger caliber weapons. The new Spectres can now acquire and destroy multiple targets simultaneously and are painted a radar invisible stealth gray color. Adding air-to-ground missiles is currently under consideration.

The 16th SOS Air Commandos have participated in actions over Panama, Grenada, El Salvador, Somalia, Iran, Iraq, Bosnia and Afghanistan. One gunship and crew were lost in Operation Desert Storm in January 1991.

Wherever there is trouble, a Spectre will be close at hand. As the squadron's motto says: "You can run, but you'll only die tired!" I am a card carrying member of the TLC Brotherhood (Thailand-Laos-Cambodia), the Air Commandos' Association and the Spectre Association...and damn proud of it. *"If you ain't Spectre..."*

In the early 1980s, the U. S. government was granted permission by the Laotian government to conduct joint crash-site investigations. The dense jungle area where No. 044 crashed was excavated and some bone fragments and personal effects were uncovered. A dog tag belonging to Captain Castillo, the IR operator, was found along with a pistol and a pocket knife. (The knife may have been the one from my tool box.) The team spent almost two weeks at the site, which they say had been tampered with. Most of those of my crew are still listed as MIA.

As of 2009, the U.S. government is trying desperately to convince the families that small bone fragments are those of my entire crew and attempting to close the books on the MIA in S.E. Asia. Some families have accepted the findings while others stubbornly adhere to the lack of true, concrete evidence of their loved ones. It seems almost every month now one reads of the final burial of yet another MIA from the Vietnam War. My feelings are the government is tired of paying the families and tired of the still constant stream of live sightings in Vietnam, Laos and Cambodia. It's an embarrassment to the government and they want the whole ordeal swept away. Read the book *An Enormous Crime*, by Bill Hendon, and see if you come away believing what our government tells us about this issue.

The area southwest of Hue in South Vietnam where No. 043 crashed was also excavated with mixed results. Again, rumors persist to this day that some in that crew are still alive and have been seen held captive. Sergeant Mercer is foremost among them. May God have mercy on those in our government, who have sat on their hands for over forty-five years refusing to believe the evidence indicating that live Americans are still being held captive.

Lately, I've been exploring the Internet and opening up communicating with old friends. Most recently, I ran across Sgt. Bob Wollman (571), fellow Spectre crew chief, and discovered we live only ten minutes from each other. We've been this close for thirty years, and neither one of us knew it. Bob and I have gotten together a number of times and were filmed once by a TV crew re-enacting our first reunion. The short film ran on the television news over the 4th of July holiday. A few weeks later, Bob made calls to Air Force people here and in Florida. Through his efforts we received a guided tour on a Spectre gunship TDY to joint base Lewis-McChord, in Tacoma. The timing was perfect and the memories were priceless. Thank you Bob, for your enduring friendship.

Bob, in fact, directed me to an Internet site that allowed me to discover another friend and fellow crew chief—none other than John Forsberg! I knew he was from somewhere in Connecticut, but that was all. Through an Internet locater site I was able to come up with his address and phone number. It took me a few hours to muster up the courage to sit and dial his number.

"Hello?" A very low voice answered. Exhaling slowly I asked, "Is this the same John Forsberg that was a C-130 crew chief in the Air Force serving at Dyess AFB and with Spectre in Thailand in the late '60s and early '70s?

After a seemingly long pause I heard a loud gasp. "Oh, my God!"

"John, this is Tom Combs calling from Seattle, Washington. Is that really you"? I asked. His voice was different, but the accent and the way he laughed was vintage Forsberg. Since then we have spoken a few times and written often. I am indebted to my friend, John, for his many photos, sent to me from clear across the country for inclusion in this effort. But most of all thank you, John, for remembering me with the same affection I have felt for you all these years. I told John on the phone that years ago I had a dream in which he had died. It was scary and felt real, and had put me in a funk for a long while. Just hearing his voice again was a giant relief!

Just recently, I have established contact with Dan O'Neill as well. He lives in Wisconsin and is caring for a large family. Perhaps we'll entice him to come out West for a visit sometime. I found Dan's comments on a C-130 web site and immediately e-mailed him, and we've been sharing information ever since. What a thrill it is to hear from him!

John Rhett lives about an hour away and we speak on the phone and visit periodically. We finally forged a small reunion at John Rhett's home, and have since gotten together a few times. Sergeants Rhett, Wollman and Combs together again!

And yes, Sgt. Forsberg finally made a trip out West. I had always looked forward to the day we would all stand together share a few beers and embrace—crew chiefs together again after forty-four years. John Forsberg was just as I had remembered him, full of joy and spirit.

Just a few months prior to one of our get-togethers, Bob Wollman was able to connect me with his assistant crew chief on aircraft 571. Sergeant John Schrawder is a sheriff in Pennsylvania. He is married with children, and was quite pleased to connect. We exchanged numerous e-mails and numerous memories of our time together. In fact it was John Schrawder that informed me of the final burial of Sgt. Caniford's remains at Arlington National Cemetery on June 17, 2010. A large monument was erected for the unidentified remains of Spectre 13. I wrote a personal letter to Caniford's family detailing the last night as they departed Ubon on their ill-fated mission. Bless his heart, John and his wife Theresa packed up and made the trip to Arlington and personally delivered my letter to Caniford's family at the gravesite. I am forever grateful for this special mission of compassion on behalf of my fallen crew. Tragically, only four months later, John Schrawder suffered a massive heart attack and died. His final act of courage, compassion and patriotism will stay with me all the rest of my days. Another fellow Spectre gone...

Not long ago I received a phone call from a woman in Texas. "This is Nell Miller-Smith," she said. "Captain Curtis Miller was my son. His airplane was shot down over Laos in March 1972. He is still missing in action." Now it was my turn to be stunned. I was talking to my copilot's mother. She tracked me down from an old letter I had written to the Department of the Air Force asking for information about my gunship and crew. She and I spoke for over an hour that night and cried numerous times. Captain Miller's little daughter is grown and recently married. His wife has not re-married nor dated all these years. His father died broken hearted just two years after the shoot down. Nell has remarried. She has been relentless in her pursuit from the government for information about her son. Still today, there is no positive proof one way or the other whether her son and many others are dead or captive. Nell and I have shared photos and stories. She leaves her porch light on every night... just in case. I treasure our newly found friendship.

Now multiply her tragedy thirteen times (for the remaining crewmen of Spectre 13) and you begin to understand the scope of sorrow that resulted. Add another eleven stories of widows and orphaned children that was the result of Zero Four Three's shoot-down in June. For me personally, that's what I'll take from the experience. The terrible waste of human lives for a cause we had all but given up on. Just like the free-spinning props of my C-130 after engine shut-down. As the turbines wound down, the props spun into a visible and lethal cutting blade. For me it was like that in 1972. The engines of America's war machine had basically been shut down. However, our gunships and many others continued the fight as troops were being withdrawn and squadrons rotated home. That good men died and families were irreparably damaged during this time in the war makes it all the harder to swallow. Peripherally, that's my burden as the crew chief of gunships 043 and 044.

Place this in the dimensions of millions on all sides and you begin to see the upfront in-your-face reality of war and what it does to the societies of both the victor and the vanquished. Today with the aid of the Internet, I'm able to touch upon the lives of many fellow soldiers. There are thousands of stories yet to be told and the Internet is a useful forum to share these experiences. I find it very interesting also that now in the year 2017 many evaders of the Vietnam War are claiming to have served. They share their stories of bravery and medals, yet the truth be known, they never left the safety of home nor wore the uniform of our country's services. Shame, shame on you!

Most recently, I have corresponded with Robert Ramsower. Robert is the brother of Major Irving Ramsower, my gallant pilot lost with Spectre 13. He has been a source of vital information regarding the crew and their families. Robert has been instrumental in my getting this story published. I can't thank you enough! He also put me in touch with Chip Halpin, the brother of Dick Halpin. Chip also served in the Air Force and was stationed in Europe when he received the news of his brother's shoot-down. I am forever grateful for the guidance and wisdom from these family members. Further, Robert put me in touch with a friend of his named Larry Phillips. Larry has enjoyed a career in journalism and possesses a keen eye. He has proofread my entire manuscript, and helped make it what it is today. Thank you so very much Larry for your valuable expertise. Clearly, I could not have accomplished this task alone.

I wish to offer additional acknowledgment to the individuals that offered time and special treasure towards my pursuit in having my manuscript published. I could not have done this without the abiding support from my darling wife, Ruth, and my stepson, Jason. My brothers John Combs and Mike Combs also made this possible. And love to my brother Maurie Combs. My fellow Spectre crew chief Bob Wollman offered assistance and treasure. Robert Ramsower and his sister Grace Ramsower Daubert were instrumental in seeing this project through. All of you have my eternal gratitude. Thank you from the very bottom of my heart. Finally, I wish to acknowledge Harley Patrick and his entire staff at L&R Publishing/Hellgate Press. Your highest level of professionalism from the very beginning has made this journey smooth and enjoyable. Thank you for bringing my story to print.

Another interesting and entertaining aspect of the computer application in the writing of this book has been in flight simulations. I can now power up a computer game to "fly" AC 130 gunship missions over Vietnam. I am able to perform as an entire crew, piloting in the darkness to the target area then using sensors to locate targets. Switching between my 20mm guns to my 105mm big gun, I fire upon my weary target far below while avoiding Triple-A and SAMs. Big difference when I get shot down though...I get to start all over again. Reality is not so forgiving. Still, I find an odd comfort alone in my room flying midnight missions over the Ho Chi Minh Trail.

During the war, crews went to great lengths to attempt recovery of downed Airmen. Many times more lives were lost than recovered, but we made the efforts just the same. I know...I was there. I firmly believe deep down inside my soul, that our government left many behind still alive. Some of those were comrades and friends of mine. It still hurts. Without a doubt, it always will.

John Forsberg (*right*) traveled on motorcycle clear across the country from Connecticut to Washington for a crew chief reunion. I had not been with John since that day on the Ubon flight line as we stood, soaking wet, saying our goodbyes. Compare this photo with that of the early days at Dyess AFB in 1970. John has gotten older while I look the same!

Spectre Crew Chiefs Reunion, 2015. *Left to right:*
Bob Wollman, me, John Rhett and John Forsberg.
Together again after forty-four years. I am forever
grateful for the enduring friendships from these
men. Ahhh the memories.

Combs Brothers, 2017. *Left to right*: Michael, John, me and Maurie. Each of
my brothers played a small part in my Air Force experiences. I love you!

Still playing after all these years! I enjoy the music, the friendships and the fun we have together. Brian Greene, Reed Keagle, John Gustoveson and yours truly comprise the classic rock group SUDDEN DOWNPOUR.

This journey started all those years ago at NKP with Fred Marshall's inspiration. Currently, I am a senior ranking black belt in Goju karate.

Two headstones at Arlington National Cemetery. *Top*: Spectre 044, I will remember these brave men every day of my life. I am honored to have served with you. *Bottom*: Spectre 043. Another reminder of the courage and sacrifice I witnessed by the brave aircrews of Spectre. You will never be forgotten. It has been my privilege to have served among you.

www.hellgatepress.com

CPSIA Information can be obtained
at www.ICGtesting.com
Printed in the USA
BVHW040619220821
614831BV00008B/104/J